OFFICIAL SQA PAST PAPERS
WITH ANSWERS

ADVANCED HIGHER

CHEMISTRY
2009-2013

HODDER
GIBSON
LEARN MORE

Hodder Gibson is grateful to the copyright holders, as credited on the final page of the Question Section, for permission to use their material. Every effort has been made to trace the copyright holders and to obtain their permission for the use of copyright material. Hodder Gibson will be happy to receive information allowing us to rectify any error or omission in future editions.

Hachette UK's policy is to use papers that are natural, renewable and recyclable products and made from wood grown in sustainable forests. The logging and manufacturing processes are expected to conform to the environmental regulations of the country of origin.

Orders: please contact Bookpoint Ltd, 130 Park Drive, Abingdon, Oxon OX14 4SE. Telephone: (44) 01235 827720. Fax: (44) 01235 400454.

Lines are open 9.00–5.00, Monday to Saturday, with a 24-hour message answering service. Visit our website at www.hoddereducation.co.uk. Hodder Gibson can be contacted direct on: Tel: 0141 848 1609; Fax: 0141 889 6315; email: hoddergibson@hodder.co.uk

This collection first published in 2013 by

Hodder Gibson, an imprint of Hodder Education,

An Hachette UK Company

2a Christie Street

Paisley PA1 1NB

Hodder Gibson is grateful to Bright Red Publishing Ltd for collaborative work in preparation of this book and all SQA Past Paper and National 5 Model Paper titles 2013.

Typeset by PDQ Digital Media Solutions Ltd, Bungay, Suffolk NR35 1BY

Printed in the UK

A catalogue record for this title is available from the British Library

ISBN 978-1-4718-0307-9

3 2 1

2014 2013

Introduction

Study Skills – what you need to know to pass exams!

Pause for thought

Many students might skip quickly through a page like this. After all, we all know how to revise. Do you really though?

Think about this:

"IF YOU ALWAYS DO WHAT YOU ALWAYS DO, YOU WILL ALWAYS GET WHAT YOU HAVE ALWAYS GOT."

Do you like the grades you get? Do you want to do better? If you get full marks in your assessment, then that's great! Change nothing! This section is just to help you get that little bit better than you already are.

There are two main parts to the advice on offer here. The first part highlights fairly obvious things but which are also very important. The second part makes suggestions about revision that you might not have thought about but which WILL help you.

Part 1

DOH! It's so obvious but …

Start revising in good time

Don't leave it until the last minute – this will make you panic.

Make a revision timetable that sets out work time AND play time.

Sleep and eat!

Obvious really, and very helpful. Avoid arguments or stressful things too – even games that wind you up. You need to be fit, awake and focused!

Know your place!

Make sure you know exactly **WHEN and WHERE** your exams are.

Know your enemy!

Make sure you know what to expect in the exam.

How is the paper structured?

How much time is there for each question?

What types of question are involved?

Which topics seem to come up time and time again?

Which topics are your strongest and which are your weakest?

Are all topics compulsory or are there choices?

Learn by DOING!

There is no substitute for past papers and practice papers – they are simply essential! Tackling this collection of papers and answers is exactly the right thing to be doing as your exams approach.

Part 2

People learn in different ways. Some like low light, some bright. Some like early morning, some like evening / night. Some prefer warm, some prefer cold. But everyone uses their BRAIN and the brain works when it is active. Passive learning – sitting gazing at notes – is the most INEFFICIENT way to learn anything. Below you will find tips and ideas for making your revision more effective and maybe even more enjoyable. What follows gets your brain active, and active learning works!

Activity 1 – Stop and review

Step 1

When you have done no more than 5 minutes of revision reading STOP!

Step 2

Write a heading in your own words which sums up the topic you have been revising.

Step 3

Write a summary of what you have revised in no more than two sentences. Don't fool yourself by saying, 'I know it but I cannot put it into words'. That just means you don't know it well enough. If you cannot write your summary, revise that section again, knowing that you must write a summary at the end of it. Many of you will have notebooks full of blue/black ink writing. Many of the pages will not be especially attractive or memorable so try to liven them up a bit with colour as you are reviewing and rewriting. **This is a great memory aid, and memory is the most important thing.**

Activity 2 — Use technology!

Why should everything be written down? Have you thought about 'mental' maps, diagrams, cartoons and colour to help you learn? And rather than write down notes, why not record your revision material?

What about having a text message revision session with friends? Keep in touch with them to find out how and what they are revising and share ideas and questions.

Why not make a video diary where you tell the camera what you are doing, what you think you have learned and what you still have to do? No one has to see or hear it but the process of having to organise your thoughts in a formal way to explain something is a very important learning practice.

Be sure to make use of electronic files. You could begin to summarise your class notes. Your typing might be slow but it will get faster and the typed notes will be easier to read than the scribbles in your class notes. Try to add different fonts and colours to make your work stand out. You can easily Google relevant pictures, cartoons and diagrams which you can copy and paste to make your work more attractive and **MEMORABLE**.

Activity 3 – This is it. Do this and you will know lots!

Step 1

In this task you must be very honest with yourself! Find the SQA syllabus for your subject (www.sqa.org.uk). Look at how it is broken down into main topics called MANDATORY knowledge. That means stuff you MUST know.

Step 2

BEFORE you do ANY revision on this topic, write a list of everything that you already know about the subject. It might be quite a long list but you only need to write it once. It shows you all the information that is already in your long-term memory so you know what parts you do not need to revise!

Step 3

Pick a chapter or section from your book or revision notes. Choose a fairly large section or a whole chapter to get the most out of this activity.

With a buddy, use Skype, Facetime, Twitter or any other communication you have, to play the game "If this is the answer, what is the question?". For example, if you are revising Geography and the answer you provide is "meander", your buddy would have to make up a question like "What is the word that describes a feature of a river where it flows slowly and bends often from side to side?".

Make up 10 "answers" based on the content of the chapter or section you are using. Give this to your buddy to solve while you solve theirs.

Step 4

Construct a wordsearch of at least 10 X 10 squares. You can make it as big as you like but keep it realistic. Work together with a group of friends. Many apps allow you to make wordsearch puzzles online. The words and phrases can go in any direction and phrases can be split. Your puzzle must only contain facts linked to the topic you are revising. Your task is to find 10 bits of information to hide in your puzzle but you must not repeat information that you used in Step 3. DO NOT show where the words are. Fill up empty squares with random letters. Remember to keep a note of where your answers are hidden but do not show your friends. When you have a complete puzzle, exchange it with a friend to solve each other's puzzle.

Step 5

Now make up 10 questions (not "answers" this time) based on the same chapter used in the previous two tasks. Again, you must find NEW information that you have not yet used. Now it's getting hard to find that new information! Again, give your questions to a friend to answer.

Step 6

As you have been doing the puzzles, your brain has been actively searching for new information. Now write a NEW LIST that contains only the new information you have discovered when doing the puzzles. Your new list is the one to look at repeatedly for short bursts over the next few days. Try to remember more and more of it without looking at it. After a few days, you should be able to add words from your second list to your first list as you increase the information in your long-term memory.

FINALLY! Be inspired...

Make a list of different revision ideas and beside each one write **THINGS I HAVE** tried, **THINGS I WILL** try and **THINGS I MIGHT** try. Don't be scared of trying something new.

And remember – "FAIL TO PREPARE AND PREPARE TO FAIL!"

Advanced Higher Chemistry

The course

The Advanced Higher Chemistry course develops the candidate's knowledge and understanding of the physical and natural environments. The Advanced Higher course builds on the Higher course and develops further the underlying theories of chemistry and the practical skills used in chemistry laboratories. The course offers candidates, in an interesting and enjoyable manner, an enhanced awareness of what chemistry is all about.

The course is designed to allow candidates to develop:

- knowledge and understanding of chemical theories and principles
- the ability to solve problems in chemistry
- the ability to carry out advanced practical work including a chemical investigation
- skills of independent study and research
- the ability to analyse experimental information and draw valid conclusions.

The course has three theoretical units which are Organic Chemistry, Principles of Chemical Reactions (Physical Chemistry) and Electronic Structure and the Periodic Table (Inorganic Chemistry). There are also 12 Prescribed Practical Activities (PPAs) to do as well as a practical Chemical Investigation.

How the course is graded

The grade you finally get for Advanced Higher Chemistry depends on three things:

- the internal assessments you do in school or college (the "NABs") – these don't count towards the final grade, but you must have passed them before you can achieve a final grade. There are four NABs that you need to pass, including one on the Chemical Investigation. This one is assessed by your teacher/ tutor checking your day book at regular intervals during the time you are carrying out your Investigation
- the examination you sit in May/June
- your investigation report which has to be sent to the SQA by a certain date in April and is marked by a specialist.

The examination

The external examination is a 2½ hour paper with a total of 100 marks. It consists of two sections. Section A has 40 multiple choice items and Section B has extended response questions totalling 60 marks. The questions are designed to test knowledge and understanding as well as problem solving.

In total the number of marks testing knowledge and understanding is slightly greater than the number of marks assessing problem solving skills.

The problem solving skills assessed in the examination include:

- selecting and presenting information
- carrying out calculations
- planning, designing and evaluating experimental procedures
- drawing conclusions and giving explanations
- making generalisations and predictions.

The Investigation report

This is marked out of 25 marks and the marking is broken down into different categories.

- Presentation (3 marks)
- Underlying Chemistry (4 marks)
- Procedures (6 marks)
- Results (5 marks)
- Conclusions and Evaluation (7 marks)

Each year a new guide for candidates is produced and can be downloaded from the SQA website. It is very important that you use the most up-to-date version of this guide since it gives very useful information on how to write up your report. Markers comment every year about how poorly some candidates do because they have not followed the advice given in the guide.

For session 2012/13 the candidates' guide was located at http://www.sqa.org.uk/sqa/files_ccc/2013_Chemistry_ Advanced-Higher_Investigation-Guidance.pdf

Preparation and hints

Keep practising multiple choice questions from Section A and going over the answers given in this book. You should also find past papers from previous years and make sure you can work out the correct answers. You will also see that some types of questions appear more often than others.

In Section B there are some questions that require only one word answers but there are also ones that require an explanation. In these questions make sure your explanation is clear and you should read over your answer after you have written it to ensure it makes sense.

Remember spelling of names of compounds can be very important in chemistry and this is probably most important at Advanced Higher level. Make sure you write clearly so that it is easy for the marker to distinguish between the letters "o", "e" and "a" so that it is clear whether you are writing alkenes or alkanes and alkanols or alkanals, for example. You should also make sure you write lower case,"k" and upper case "K" so that it is obvious which one you mean. For example, the symbol for the rate constant is k (lower case) and the symbol K is the symbol for potassium or for Kelvins or for the equilibrium constant.

The number of marks for calculations in the exam is usually around 25 out of the total 100 marks and you must have a scientific calculator so that you can use the log button for pH calculations.

Remember to make connections between parts of questions, particularly where there are three or four parts to a question. These are almost always linked and, in some instances, an earlier answer in part (a) or (b) is needed. Very often in the last question of section B, you are given information which should help you identify a compound. For example, you may have to work out the empirical formula and the molecular formula of the substance and then continue using information from, say, infra-red and proton nmr spectra to finally identify it. To do this you need to use all the information given and your answers to previous parts of the question, not just the information given in the final part. Below are some more key tips for your success.

Accuracy and Units

In your final answer in a calculation do not put in too many significant figures. In most cases three significant figures is adequate. It is fine to have a lot of significant figures during the calculation but avoid putting in too many in the final answer. You may lose marks for too many significant figures in the final answer. Make sure your final answer in a calculation has the correct units. If you are asked to calculate $\Delta G°$ in kJ mol^{-1}, then leaving an answer in J or J mol^{-1} will lose a mark. Make sure you show steps clearly in a calculation so that if your final answer is wrong then the marker may be able to award partial marks if your working is easy to understand.

Chemical Relationships

There are certain relationships you are expected to know and be able to apply at Advanced Higher level. Examples include $pH = -\log[H^+]$ and $pH = \frac{1}{2} pK_a - \frac{1}{2} \log c$ and $\Delta Go = \Delta Ho - T\Delta So$ but there are a few others that you need to know. You will get a mark for writing the relationship correctly and the other marks would be for applying it correctly. You must learn all these relationships and regular practice using them in calculations will prepare you better for the examination.

Higher knowledge

In the Advanced Higher exam, there are up to 10 marks in there from the Higher Chemistry course. The first few multiple choice questions in Section A are very often from the Higher Chemistry course. You should look at these multiple choice questions and make sure you can answer them. If not then you should re-visit the relevant parts of Higher Chemistry.

Marking instructions

Ensure that you look at the detailed marking instructions of past papers. They provide further advice and guidelines as well as showing you precisely where, and for what, marks are awarded. It may be that markers would be instructed to accept other answers but, in general, the answers given in this book are what were expected by the exam setters. Also if the question is worth only one mark then you are not expected to write much – maybe only one word. You are expected to write much more for two or three mark questions. Remember there are no ½ marks awarded in Advanced Higher Chemistry so if your answer to a 1 mark question is only half correct then you get no marks. Also, if you make an error, no matter how slight, you will lose one mark. Make sure when answering "explain" type questions you don't write contradictory statements. The wrong answer will cancel out the correct one and no marks will be awarded.

Timing

You have 2½ hours to complete the exam paper. There are 100 marks in the exam paper so this works out at 1½ minutes per mark. Best to try to get through Section A in about 45 minutes leaving you more time for Section B. Don't spend too much time on each question. If you do you may find you don't manage to complete the exam paper. It is better to leave out a question worth three marks and hope to come back to it rather than spend 10 minutes on it but not have enough time to do a fairly easy question worth six marks at the end of the paper.

Chemical Investigation

Remember to download the candidates' guide from the SQA website. It cannot be stressed enough how important this is.

And finally!

Remember that the rewards for passing Advanced Higher Chemistry are well worth it! Your pass will help open doors to get the future you want for yourself. In the exam, be confident in your own ability. In Section A, if you're not sure what the correct option is, then go by your first instinct. Work through the paper at a good pace. Keep calm and don't panic! GOOD LUCK!

ADVANCED HIGHER

2009

[BLANK PAGE]

X012/701

NATIONAL
QUALIFICATIONS
2009

WEDNESDAY, 3 JUNE
9.00 AM – 11.30 AM

CHEMISTRY
ADVANCED HIGHER

Reference may be made to the Chemistry Higher and Advanced Higher Data Booklet .

SECTION A — 40 marks

Instructions for completion of **SECTION A** are given on page two.

For this section of the examination you must use an **HB pencil**.

SECTION B — 60 marks

All questions should be attempted.

Answers must be written clearly and legibly in ink.

SECTION A

Read carefully

1 Check that the answer sheet provided is for **Chemistry Advanced Higher (Section A)**.

2 For this section of the examination you must use an **HB pencil** and, where necessary, an eraser.

3 Check that the answer sheet you have been given has **your name**, **date of birth**, **SCN** (Scottish Candidate Number) and **Centre Name** printed on it.

Do not change any of these details.

4 If any of this information is wrong, tell the Invigilator immediately.

5 If this information is correct, **print** your name and seat number in the boxes provided.

6 The answer to each question is **either** A, B, C or D. Decide what your answer is, then, using your pencil, put a horizontal line in the space provided (see sample question below).

7 There is **only one correct** answer to each question.

8 Any rough working should be done on the question paper or the rough working sheet, **not** on your answer sheet.

9 At the end of the exam, put the **answer sheet for Section A inside the front cover of your answer book**.

Sample Question

To show that the ink in a ball-pen consists of a mixture of dyes, the method of separation would be

> A chromatography
>
> B fractional distillation
>
> C fractional crystallisation
>
> D filtration.

The correct answer is **A**—chromatography. The answer **A** has been clearly marked in **pencil** with a horizontal line (see below).

Changing an answer

If you decide to change your answer, carefully erase your first answer and using your pencil, fill in the answer you want. The answer below has been changed to **D**.

1. The diagram shows one of the series of lines in the hydrogen emission spectrum.

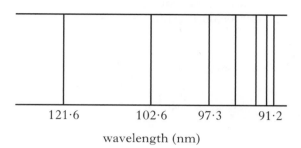

wavelength (nm)

Each line

A represents an energy level within a hydrogen atom

B results from an electron moving to a higher energy level

C lies within the visible part of the electromagnetic spectrum

D results from an excited electron dropping to a lower energy level.

2. Which of the following compounds shows most covalent character?

A CH_4

B NaH

C NH_3

D PH_3

3. In which of the following species is a dative covalent bond present?

A H_3O^+

B H_2O

C OH^-

D O_2

4. Which of the following diagrams best represents the arrangement of electron pairs around the central iodine atom in the I_3^- ion?

A   I —— I —— I

B

C

D

5. When a voltage is applied to an n-type semiconductor, which of the following migrate through the lattice?

A Electrons

B Negative ions

C Positive holes

D Both electrons and positive holes

6. Which of the following compounds would produce fumes of hydrogen chloride when added to water?

A $LiCl$

B $MgCl_2$

C PCl_3

D CCl_4

[Turn over

7. Zinc oxide reacts as shown.

$$ZnO(s) + 2HCl(aq) \rightarrow ZnCl_2(aq) + H_2O(\ell)$$

$$ZnO(s) + 2NaOH(aq) + H_2O(\ell) \rightarrow Na_2Zn(OH)_4(aq)$$

This shows that zinc oxide is

A   basic

B   acidic

C   neutral

D   amphoteric.

8. The correct formula for the tetraamminedichlorocopper(II) complex is

A $[Cu(NH_3)_4Cl_2]^{2-}$

B $[Cu(NH_3)_4Cl_2]$

C $[Cu(NH_3)_4Cl_2]^{2+}$

D $[Cu(NH_3)_4Cl_2]^{4+}$.

9. Which of the following aqueous solutions contains the **greatest** number of **negatively** charged ions?

A $500 \, cm^3$ $0.10 \, mol \, l^{-1}$ $Na_2SO_4(aq)$

B $250 \, cm^3$ $0.12 \, mol \, l^{-1}$ $BaCl_2(aq)$

C $300 \, cm^3$ $0.15 \, mol \, l^{-1}$ $KI(aq)$

D $400 \, cm^3$ $0.10 \, mol \, l^{-1}$ $Zn(NO_3)_2(aq)$

10. When one mole of phosphorus pentachloride was heated to $523 \, K$ in a closed vessel, 50% dissociated as shown.

$$PCl_5(g) \rightleftharpoons PCl_3(g) + Cl_2(g)$$

How many moles of gas were present in the equilibrium mixture?

A   0·5

B   1·0

C   1·5

D   2·0

11. Which of the following graphs shows the temperature change as $2 \, mol \, l^{-1}$ sodium hydroxide is added to $25 \, cm^3$ of $2 \, mol \, l^{-1}$ hydrochloric acid?

A

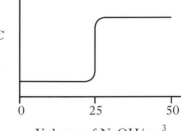

Volume of NaOH/cm^3

B

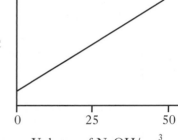

Volume of NaOH/cm^3

C

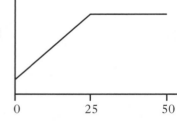

Volume of NaOH/cm^3

D

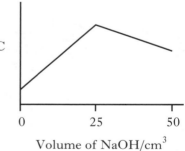

Volume of NaOH/cm^3

12. In the equilibrium $N_2O_4(g) \rightleftharpoons 2NO_2(g)$ the forward reaction is endothermic.

    Which one of the following causes an increase in the value of the equilibrium constant?

    A   The removal of NO_2

    B   An increase of pressure

    C   A decrease of temperature

    D   An increase of temperature

13. In which of the following separation techniques is partition between two separate phases **not** a part of the process?

    A   Recrystallisation of benzoic acid from hot water

    B   Separation of alkanes using gas-liquid chromatography

    C   Separation of plant dyes using paper chromatography

    D   Solvent extraction of caffeine from an aqueous solution using dichloromethane

14. An aqueous solution of an organic acid, X, was shaken with chloroform until the following equilibrium was established.

    $$X\ (water) \rightleftharpoons X\ (chloroform)$$

    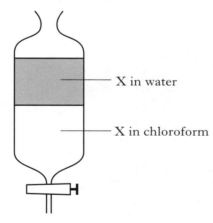

    $25 \cdot 0\,cm^3$ of the upper layer needed $20 \cdot 0\,cm^3$ of $0 \cdot 050\ mol\ l^{-1}$ NaOH(aq) for neutralisation. $25 \cdot 0\,cm^3$ of the lower layer needed $13 \cdot 3\,cm^3$ of $0 \cdot 050\ mol\ l^{-1}$ NaOH(aq) for neutralisation.

    The value of the partition coefficient is

    A $0 \cdot 67$

    B $1 \cdot 25$

    C $1 \cdot 50$

    D $1 \cdot 88$.

15. Which of the following would **not** be suitable to act as a buffer solution?

    A   Boric acid and sodium borate

    B   Nitric acid and sodium nitrate

    C   Benzoic acid and sodium benzoate

    D   Propanoic acid and sodium propanoate

16. Which of the following $0 \cdot 01\ mol\,l^{-1}$ aqueous solutions has the highest pH value?

    A   Sodium fluoride

    B   Sodium benzoate

    C   Sodium propanoate

    D   Sodium methanoate

17. Which of the following graphs shows the variation in ΔG° with temperature for a reaction which is always feasible?

    A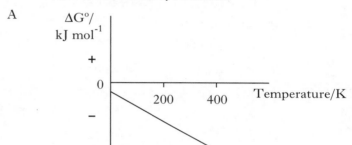

    B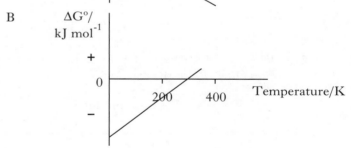

    C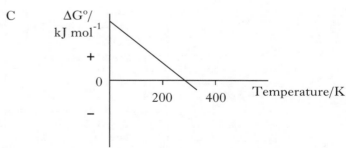

    D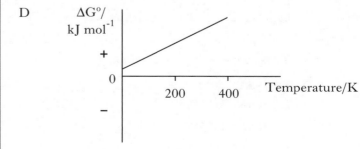

18. When water evaporates from a puddle which of the following applies?

   A ΔH positive and ΔS positive

   B ΔH positive and ΔS negative

   C ΔH negative and ΔS positive

   D ΔH negative and ΔS negative

19. For which of the following reactions would the value of $\Delta G° - \Delta H°$ be approximately zero?

   A $CaCO_3(s) \rightarrow CaO(s) + CO_2(g)$

   B $C(s) + H_2O(g) \rightarrow CO(g) + H_2(g)$

   C $Zn(s) + 2H^+(aq) \rightarrow Zn^{2+}(aq) + H_2(g)$

   D $Cu^{2+}(aq) + Mg(s) \rightarrow Mg^{2+}(aq) + Cu(s)$

20. For the reaction

   $$2NO(g) + Cl_2(g) \rightarrow 2NOCl(g)$$

   the rate equation is

   $$\text{rate} = k[NO][Cl_2].$$

   The overall order of this reaction is

   A 1

   B 2

   C 3

   D 5.

21. The following data refer to initial reaction rates obtained for the reaction

   $$X + Y + Z \rightarrow \text{products}$$

Run	Relative concentrations			Relative initial rate
	[X]	[Y]	[Z]	
1	1·0	1·0	1·0	0·3
2	1·0	2·0	1·0	0·6
3	2·0	2·0	1·0	1·2
4	2·0	1·0	2·0	0·6

   These data fit the rate equation

   A Rate = $k[X]$

   B Rate = $k[X][Y]$

   C Rate = $k[X][Y]^2$

   D Rate = $k[X][Y][Z]$

22. Which of the following is a propagation step in the chlorination of methane?

   A $Cl_2 \rightarrow Cl\bullet + Cl\bullet$

   B $CH_3\bullet + Cl\bullet \rightarrow CH_3Cl$

   C $CH_3\bullet + Cl_2 \rightarrow CH_3Cl + Cl\bullet$

   D $CH_4 + Cl\bullet \rightarrow CH_3Cl + H\bullet$

23. The hydrolysis of the halogenoalkane $(CH_3)_3CBr$ was found to take place by an S_N1 mechanism.

   The rate-determining step involved the formation of

   A

   B

   C

   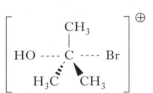

   D

   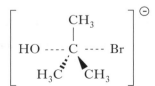

24. $OH^- + CO_2 \rightarrow HCO_3^-$

    $C_2H_4 + Br_2 \rightarrow C_2H_4Br^+ + Br^-$

    Which substances act as electrophiles in the above reactions?

    A OH^- and Br_2

    B OH^- and C_2H_4

    C CO_2 and Br_2

    D CO_2 and C_2H_4

25.

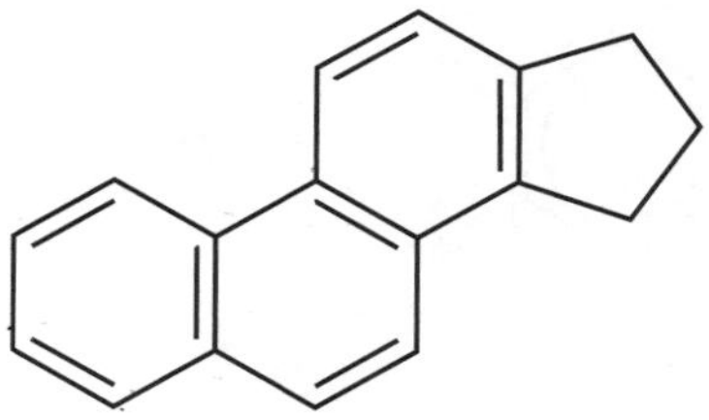

What is the molecular formula for the above structure?

A $C_{17}H_{11}$

B $C_{17}H_{14}$

C $C_{17}H_{17}$

D $C_{17}H_{20}$

26. Which line in the table is correct for the following hydrocarbon?

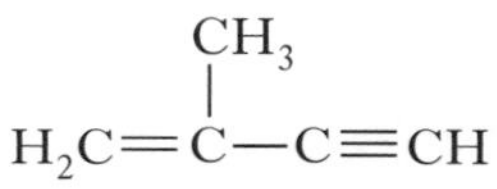

	Number of σ bonds	Number of π bonds
A	4	3
B	8	5
C	10	2
D	10	3

27. When but-2-ene is shaken with an aqueous solution of chlorine in potassium iodide, the structural formula(e) of the product(s) is/are

A

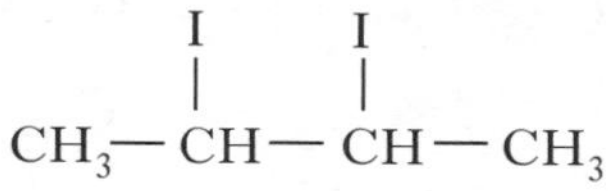

B

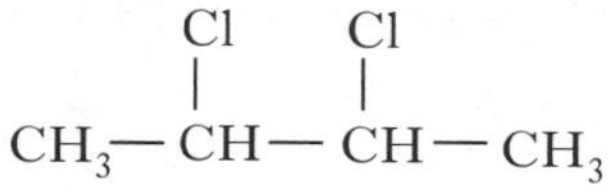

C

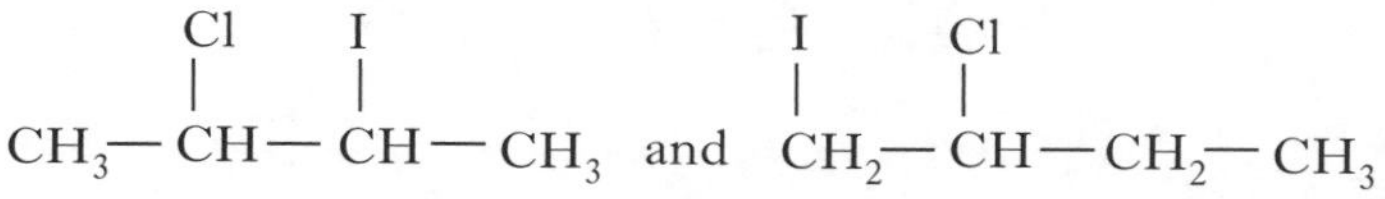

D

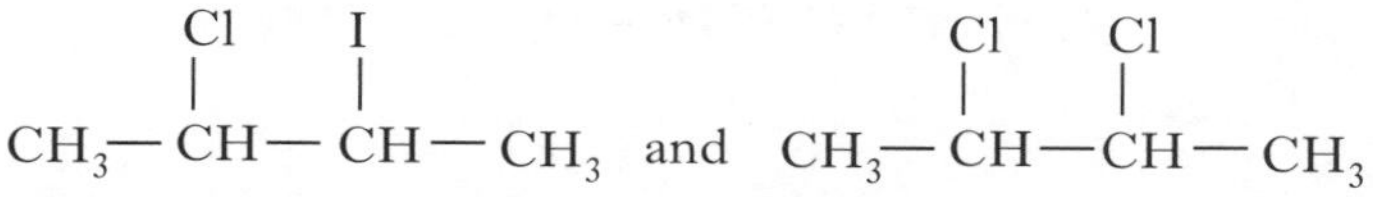

28. Which of the following reacts with ethanol to form the ethoxide ion?

    A Na(s)

    B $Na_2O(s)$

    C NaCl(aq)

    D NaOH(aq)

29. Which of the following is **not** a correct statement about ethoxyethane?

    A It burns readily in air.

    B It is isomeric with butan-2-ol.

    C It has a higher boiling point than butan-2-ol.

    D It is a very good solvent for many organic compounds.

[Turn over

30. Which of the following esters gives a secondary alcohol when hydrolysed?

A

$$(CH_3)_3C-O-\overset{\overset{\displaystyle O}{\|}}{C}-H$$

B

$$CH_3-O-\overset{\overset{\displaystyle O}{\|}}{C}-CH(CH_3)_2$$

C

$$(CH_3)_2CH-O-\overset{\overset{\displaystyle O}{\|}}{C}-CH_3$$

D

$$(CH_3)_2CHCH_2-O-\overset{\overset{\displaystyle O}{\|}}{C}-CH_3$$

31. Which of the following compounds could **not** be oxidised by acidified potassium dichromate solution?

A CH_3CH_2CHO

B CH_3CH_2COOH

C $CH_3CH_2CH_2OH$

D $CH_3CH(OH)CH_3$

32. Which of the following will react with dilute sodium hydroxide solution?

A $CH_3CHOHCH_3$

B $CH_3CH=CH_2$

C CH_3COOCH_3

D $CH_3CH_2OCH_3$

33. Which of the following molecules is planar?

A Hexane

B Cyclohexane

C Chlorobenzene

D Methylbenzene (toluene)

34. Which of the following compounds is soluble in water and reacts with both dilute hydrochloric acid and sodium hydroxide solution?

A $C_2H_5NH_2$

B $C_6H_5NH_2$

C $C_2H_5NH_3Cl$

D $HOOCCH_2NH_2$

35. Which of the following reactions is least likely to take place?

A

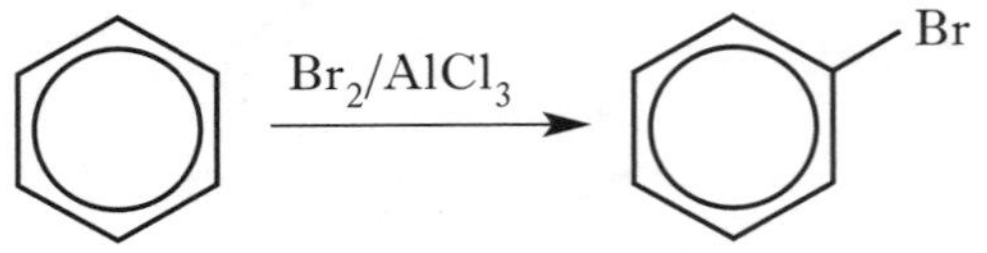

B

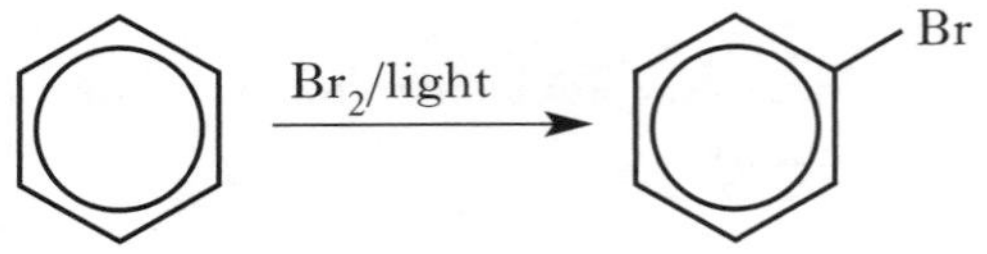

C

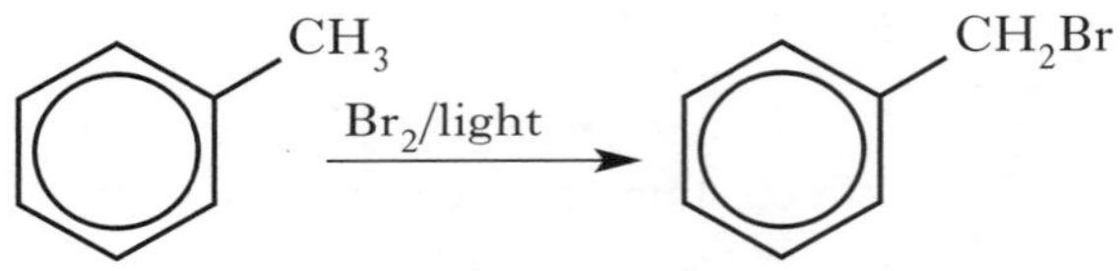

D

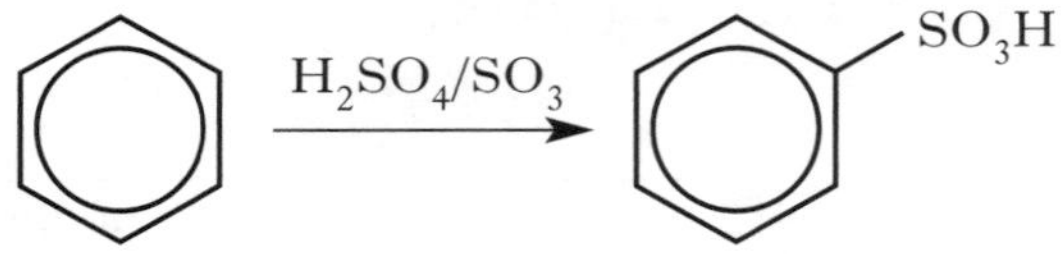

36. In which of the following pairs does an aqueous solution of the first compound have a higher pH than an aqueous solution of the second?

A 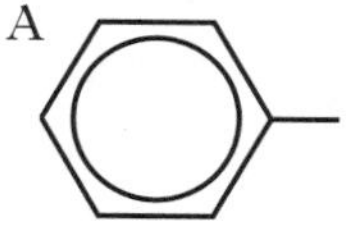 OH　and　CH_3COOH

B 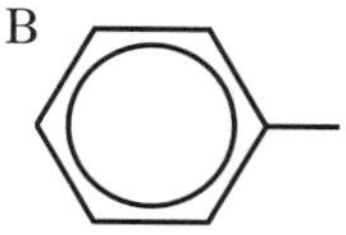 OH　and　CH_3CH_2OH

C 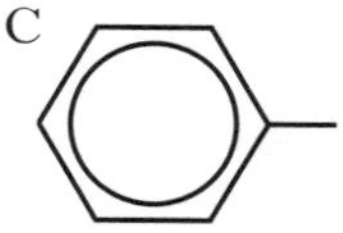 COOH　and　$HOCH_2CH_2OH$

D 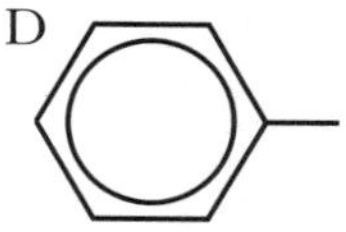 COOH　and　CH_3OH

37. Which of the following bases is the strongest?

A　$C_2H_5NH_2$

B　$(C_2H_5)_2NH$

C　$C_6H_5NH_2$

D　$(C_6H_5)_2NH$

38. Which line in the table shows a pair of optical isomers?

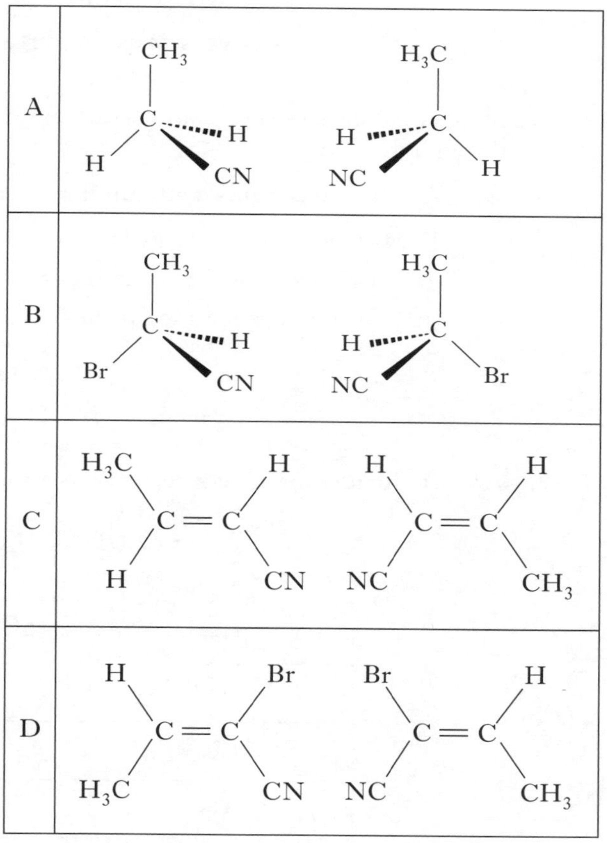

39.

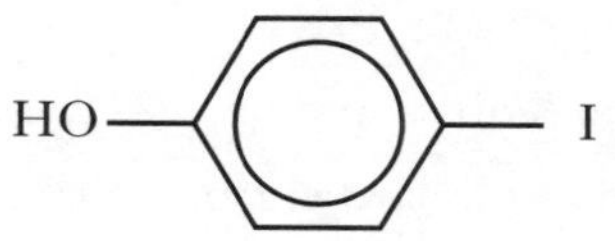

Which atom in the above structure would be located **most** readily using X-ray crystallography?

A　Carbon

B　Hydrogen

C　Iodine

D　Oxygen

40. Antihistamines act by inhibiting the action of the inflammatory agent histamine in the body.

Antihistamines can be described as

A　agonists

B　receptors

C　antagonists

D　pharmacophores.

[END OF SECTION A]

Candidates are reminded that the answer sheet for Section A MUST be placed INSIDE the front cover of your answer book.

SECTION B

60 marks are available in this section of the paper.

All answers must be written clearly and legibly in ink.

Marks

1. A detector in a Geiger counter contains argon which ionises when nuclear radiation passes through it.

   (a) Write the electronic configuration for argon in terms of s and p orbitals. **1**

   (b) The first ionisation energy of argon is $1530 \, kJ \, mol^{-1}$.

       (i) Calculate the wavelength of the radiation, in nm, corresponding to this energy. **3**

       (ii) Write the equation for the first ionisation of argon. **1**

   (5)

2. Iron(III) oxide can be reduced to iron using hydrogen.

$$Fe_2O_3(s) + 3H_2(g) \rightarrow 2Fe(s) + 3H_2O(g)$$

Substance	$\Delta H_f^\circ / kJ \, mol^{-1}$	$S^\circ / J \, K^{-1} \, mol^{-1}$
$Fe_2O_3(s)$	−822	90
$H_2(g)$	0	131
$Fe(s)$	0	27
$H_2O(g)$	−242	189

For the reduction of iron(III) oxide with hydrogen, use the data in the table to calculate

   (a) the standard entropy change, ΔS° **1**

   (b) the standard enthalpy change, ΔH° **1**

   (c) the theoretical temperature above which the reaction becomes feasible. **2**

   (4)

Marks

3. The diagram, which is not drawn to scale, represents the processes involved in a thermochemical cycle.

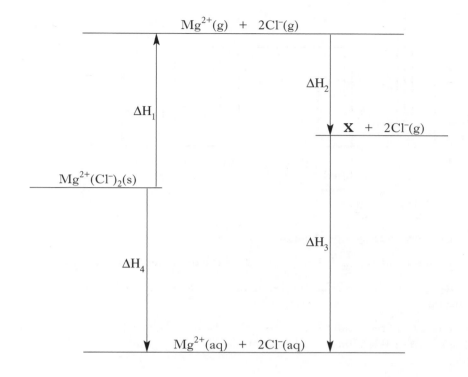

(a) What should be written in place of **X** to complete the diagram?   1

(b) What name is given to the enthalpy change represented by ΔH_1?   1

(c) Calculate ΔH_3 using information from the Data Booklet.   1

(d) Calculate ΔH_4 using information from the Data Booklet.   1

   (4)

4. (a) Using the mean bond enthalpy values given in the Data Booklet, calculate the enthalpy change, in $kJ\,mol^{-1}$, for the reaction

$$H_2(g) + \tfrac{1}{2}O_2(g) \rightarrow H_2O(g)$$

   3

(b) The value given in the Data Booklet for the standard enthalpy of combustion of hydrogen is different to that calculated in part (a).

Give the main reason for this difference.   1

   (4)

[Turn over

Marks

5.

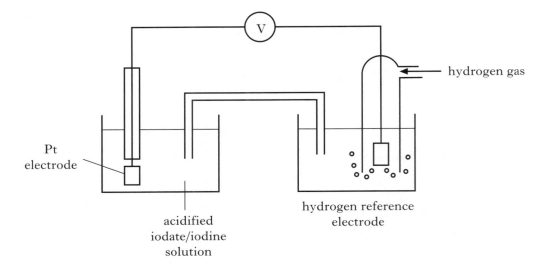

Pt electrode

acidified iodate/iodine solution

hydrogen gas

hydrogen reference electrode

The above cell was set up under standard conditions.

(a) What are the three standard conditions required for the hydrogen reference electrode?   1

(b) Write an ion-electron equation for the reduction of iodate ions (IO_3^-) to iodine (I_2) in acidic conditions.   1

(c) If the E° value for the reduction of IO_3^- to I_2 is 1·19 V, calculate the free energy change $\Delta G°$, in kJ per mole of IO_3^-, for the cell reaction.   3

(5)

6. When an ant bites, it injects methanoic acid (HCOOH).

(a) Methanoic acid is a weak acid.

$$HCOOH(aq) \; + \; H_2O(\ell) \; \rightleftharpoons \; HCOO^-(aq) \; + \; H_3O^+(aq)$$

(i) What is the conjugate base of methanoic acid?   1

(ii) Write the expression for the dissociation constant, K_a, of methanoic acid.   1

(b) (i) In a typical bite, an ant injects $3·6 \times 10^{-3}$ g of methanoic acid.
Assuming that the methanoic acid dissolves in $1·0 \text{ cm}^3$ of water in the body, calculate the concentration of the methanoic acid solution in $mol\, l^{-1}$.   2

(ii) Calculate the pH of this methanoic acid solution.   2

(6)

Marks

7. Iodine reacts with propanone as follows.

$$I_2 + CH_3COCH_3 \longrightarrow CH_3COCH_2I + HI$$

A possible mechanism for this reaction is

$$\underset{\text{CH}_3-\underset{\displaystyle\|}{\overset{\displaystyle O}{C}}-\text{CH}_3}{} + \text{H}^+ \longrightarrow \underset{\text{CH}_3-\underset{\displaystyle\|}{\overset{\displaystyle {}^+OH}{C}}-\text{CH}_3}{} \qquad \text{slow}$$

$$\underset{\text{CH}_3-\underset{\displaystyle\|}{\overset{\displaystyle {}^+OH}{C}}-\text{CH}_3}{} \longrightarrow \underset{\text{CH}_3-\underset{\displaystyle|}{\overset{\displaystyle OH}{C}}=\text{CH}_2}{} + \text{H}^+ \qquad \text{fast}$$

$$\underset{\text{CH}_3-\underset{\displaystyle|}{\overset{\displaystyle OH}{C}}=\text{CH}_2}{} + \text{I}_2 \longrightarrow \underset{\text{CH}_3-\underset{\displaystyle\|}{\overset{\displaystyle O}{C}}-\text{CH}_2\text{I}}{} + \text{HI} \qquad \text{fast}$$

(a) Write a rate equation for this reaction based on the above mechanism.   **1**

(b) What evidence indicates that the reaction is acid catalysed?   **1**

(c) In a PPA the reaction was followed by withdrawing samples at regular intervals and adding them to sodium hydrogencarbonate solution.

The concentration of iodine in these samples was then determined by titrating with a standard solution of sodium thiosulphate.

    (i) Why were the samples added to the sodium hydrogencarbonate solution?   **1**

    (ii) What indicator is used in the titration and what is the colour change at the end-point of the titration?   **1**

                                                         (4)

[Turn over

Marks

8. Nickel can be determined quantitatively in a number of ways.

   (a) The method used in a PPA is volumetric analysis in which a buffered solution of nickel(II) ions is titrated against a standard solution of a complexing agent.

   Which complexing agent is used?   1

   (b) Another way of determining nickel is by colorimetric analysis.

   Why would this be a suitable method of determining nickel(II) ions?   1

   (c) A third way of determining nickel depends on the fact that nickel(II) ions form a solid complex with butanedione dioxime.

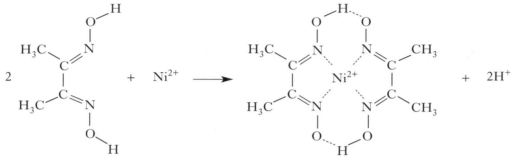

   butanedione dioxime   insoluble complex

   Using this method, a sample of a nickel(II) salt was accurately weighed and dissolved in water. To this solution, excess butanedione dioxime solution was added. The solid complex formed was filtered, washed and then heated in an oven to constant mass.

   (i) Butanedione dioxime can act as a ligand.

   What property of butanedione dioxime allows it to act as a ligand?   1

   (ii) What is the coordination number of the nickel(II) ion in the insoluble complex?   1

   (iii) Which type of quantitative analysis has been carried out using this method?   1

   (iv) During the process of heating to constant mass, the solid complex is cooled in a desiccator.

   Why is a desiccator used?   1

   (6)

Marks

9. Compound **W** reacts in two steps to form compound **Y**.

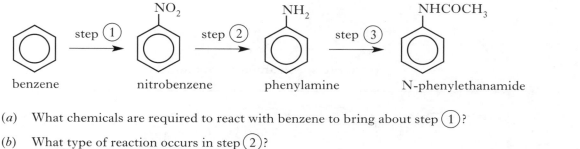

$$C_4H_9Br \xrightarrow{\;\;(1)\;\;} C_4H_{10}O \xrightarrow{\;\;(2)\;\;} C_4H_8O$$

$$\text{W} \qquad\qquad\qquad \text{X} \qquad\qquad\qquad \text{Y}$$

Y reacts with 2,4-dinitrophenylhydrazine solution (Brady's reagent) to form a yellow precipitate **Z**.

Y does not react with Fehling's solution, nor with Tollens' reagent.

(a) Identify compound **Y**.   1

(b) What type of reaction is occurring in step ①?   1

(c) What property of the yellow precipitate **Z** is measured and how is this used to confirm the identity of **Y**?   1

(d) Dehydration of compound **X** produces three unsaturated isomers of molecular formula C_4H_8. Two of these are **geometric** isomers.

Draw the structures of both **geometric** isomers and name each one.   2

    (5)

10. N-Phenylethanamide can be prepared from benzene in three steps.

benzene $\xrightarrow{\text{step }①}$ nitrobenzene $\xrightarrow{\text{step }②}$ phenylamine $\xrightarrow{\text{step }③}$ N-phenylethanamide

(a) What chemicals are required to react with benzene to bring about step ①?   1

(b) What type of reaction occurs in step ②?   1

(c) Suggest a reagent which could be used to bring about step ③.   1

    (3)

[Turn over

11. Spectra of an organic compound **A** are shown below.

Mass spectrum of compound A

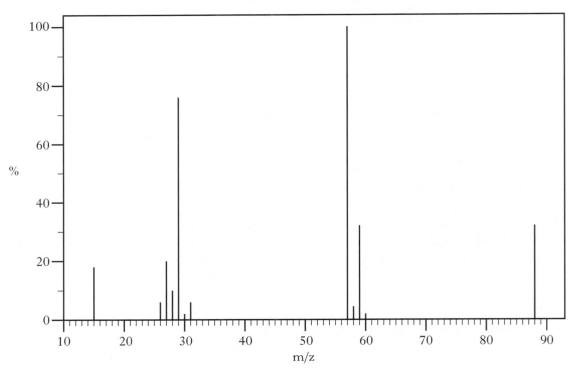

Infra-red spectrum of compound A

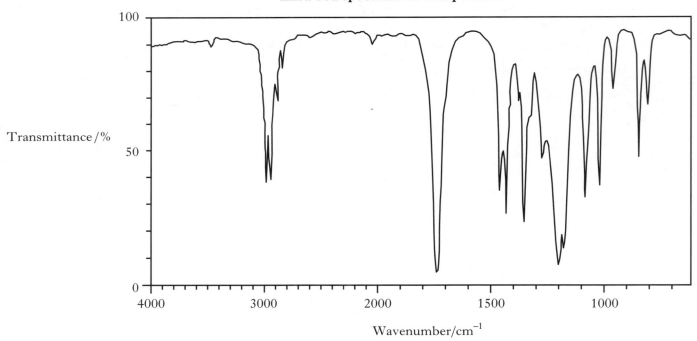

Marks

11. **(continued)**

Proton nmr spectrum of compound A

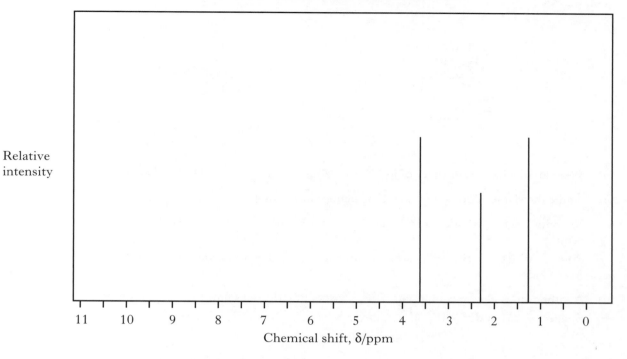

(a) Compound **A** has empirical formula C_2H_4O.

Using this information and the mass spectrum, deduce the molecular formula of **A**.   1

(b) The absorption peak at $1745\ cm^{-1}$ in the infra-red spectrum can be used to help identify **A**.

   (i)   Which bond is responsible for this absorption?   1

   (ii) Which type of compound is **A**?   1

(c) Draw the structure of the ion fragment responsible for the peak at m/z 57 in the mass spectrum.   1

(d) Considering all the evidence, including the proton nmr spectrum, name compound **A**.   1

(5)

[Turn over

Marks

12. Many interhalogen compounds exist. Two of these are iodine pentafluoride and iodine heptafluoride.

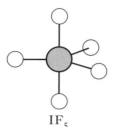 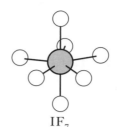

IF$_5$ IF$_7$

(a) What are the oxidation states of iodine in iodine pentafluoride and iodine heptafluoride?   **1**

(b) Name the shape adopted by the iodine pentafluoride molecule.   **1**

(c) In iodine heptafluoride, there are seven I–F bonds in which iodine uses sp^{3}d^3 hybrid orbitals.

Suggest which hybrid orbitals iodine uses in iodine pentafluoride, in which there are five I–F bonds.   **1**

(d) Another interhalogen compound, ClF$_5$, exists but ClF$_7$ does not.

Suggest a reason why ClF$_7$ does not exist.   **1**

   (4)

Marks

13. A superconductor, **X**, with a critical temperature of 95 K, was prepared by heating yttrium oxide, barium carbonate and copper oxide at high temperatures.

(a) Copy the axes shown and sketch a graph to show how the **electrical resistance** of **X** varies with temperature.

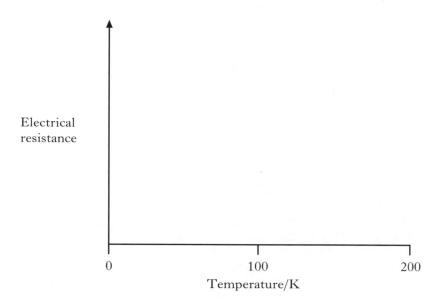

1

(b) (i) **X** contains 13·4% yttrium, 41·2% barium, 28·6% copper and 16·8% oxygen.

Assuming that the relative atomic mass of yttrium is 88·9, show by calculation that the empirical formula for **X** is $YBa_2Cu_3O_7$.

2

(ii) Assuming that the oxidation states of yttrium, barium and oxygen are +3, +2 and −2 respectively, calculate the **average** oxidation state of copper in **X**.

1

(iii) When all the copper(III) initially present in **X** is reduced to copper(II), compound **Z** is produced. The oxidation states of the other three elements do not change nor does the mole ratio of the **metals**.

Suggest an empirical formula for **Z**.

1

(5)

[*END OF QUESTION PAPER*]

[BLANK PAGE]

ADVANCED HIGHER

2010

[BLANK PAGE]

X012/701

NATIONAL QUALIFICATIONS 2010

WEDNESDAY, 2 JUNE 9.00 AM – 11.30 AM

CHEMISTRY ADVANCED HIGHER

Reference may be made to the Chemistry Higher and Advanced Higher Data Booklet.

SECTION A – 40 marks

Instructions for completion of **SECTION A** are given on page two.

For this section of the examination you must use an **HB pencil**.

SECTION B – 60 marks

All questions should be attempted.

Answers must be written clearly and legibly in ink.

SECTION A

Read carefully

1 Check that the answer sheet provided is for **Chemistry Advanced Higher (Section A)**.

2 For this section of the examination you must use an **HB pencil** and, where necessary, an eraser.

3 Check that the answer sheet you have been given has **your name**, **date of birth**, **SCN** (Scottish Candidate Number) and **Centre Name** printed on it.

Do not change any of these details.

4 If any of this information is wrong, tell the Invigilator immediately.

5 If this information is correct, **print** your name and seat number in the boxes provided.

6 The answer to each question is **either** A, B, C or D. Decide what your answer is, then, using your pencil, put a horizontal line in the space provided (see sample question below).

7 There is **only one correct** answer to each question.

8 Any rough working should be done on the question paper or the rough working sheet, **not** on your answer sheet.

9 At the end of the examination, put the **answer sheet for Section A inside the front cover of your answer book**.

Sample Question

To show that the ink in a ball-pen consists of a mixture of dyes, the method of separation would be

    A chromatography

    B fractional distillation

    C fractional crystallisation

    D filtration.

The correct answer is **A**—chromatography. The answer **A** has been clearly marked in **pencil** with a horizontal line (see below).

Changing an answer

If you decide to change your answer, carefully erase your first answer and using your pencil, fill in the answer you want. The answer below has been changed to **D**.

1. An atom of iron contains 26 electrons.

   Which of the following diagrams below correctly represents the distribution of electrons in the 3d and 4s orbitals in an atom of iron in its ground state?

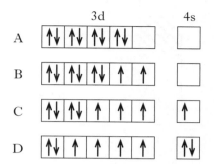

2. An atom has the electronic configuration
   $$1s^2 2s^2 2p^6 3s^2 3p^1$$

   What is the charge on the most probable ion formed by this element?

   A +1

   B +2

   C +3

   D +4

3. According to the aufbau principle, electrons fill orbitals in the order

   A 1s 2s 2p 3s 3p 4s 4p 3d

   B 1s 2s 2p 3s 3d 3p 4s 4p

   C 1s 2s 2p 3s 3p 3d 4s 4p

   D 1s 2s 2p 3s 3p 4s 3d 4p.

4. Which line in the graph represents the trend in successive ionisation energies of a Group 2 element?

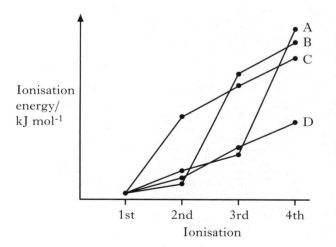

5. Which of the following statements about atomic emission spectroscopy is **incorrect**?

   A Each element provides a characteristic spectrum.

   B Visible light is used to promote electrons to higher energy levels.

   C The lines arise from electron transitions between one energy level and another.

   D The quantity of the element can be determined from the intensity of radiation transmitted.

6. Which of the following diagrams best represents the arrangement of atoms in the IF_4^- ion?

   Note: a lone pair of electrons is represented by ••

   A

   B

   C

   D

[Turn over

7. Which of the following solids is likely to have the same type of crystal lattice structure as caesium chloride?

   A $Ba^{2+}O^{2-}$

   B $Fe^{2+}O^{2-}$

   C Ag^+I^-

   D $Ni^{2+}O^{2-}$

8. An ionic hydride is added to water.

   Which line in the table correctly describes the gas produced and the type of solution formed?

	Gas produced	Type of solution formed
A	hydrogen	acidic
B	hydrogen	alkaline
C	oxygen	acidic
D	oxygen	alkaline

9. An element forms an oxide which is a gas at room temperature.

   Which type of bonding is likely to be present in the element?

   A Ionic

   B Metallic

   C Polar covalent

   D Non-polar covalent

10. Which of the following oxides would produce the solution with the greatest conductivity when 0·1 mol is added to 250 cm³ of water?

   A SO_2

   B CO_2

   C Na_2O

   D Al_2O_3

11. $2NH_3(g) \rightleftharpoons N_2(g) + 3H_2(g)$ $\Delta H^\circ = 92\,kJ\,mol^{-1}$

   The conditions favouring the decomposition of ammonia are

   A low pressure and low temperature

   B high pressure and low temperature

   C low pressure and high temperature

   D high pressure and high temperature.

12. An aqueous solution of iodine was shaken with cyclohexane until equilibrium was established.

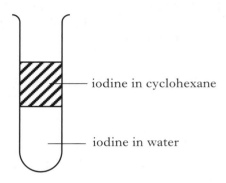
— iodine in cyclohexane
— iodine in water

   Some solid iodine was added to the test tube and the contents shaken until equilibrium was re-established.

   Which line in the table shows the effects caused by the addition of the solid iodine?

	Concentration of iodine in water	Concentration of iodine in cyclohexane	Partition coefficient
A	increases	increases	no change
B	increases	increases	increases
C	no change	increases	no change
D	increases	no change	increases

13. An acid is a substance which

   A donates a proton leaving a conjugate acid

   B donates a proton leaving a conjugate base

   C accepts a proton leaving a conjugate acid

   D accepts a proton leaving a conjugate base.

14. The pH ranges over which some indicators change colour are shown below.

   Which line in the table shows the indicator most suitable for the titration of hydrochloric acid with ammonia solution?

	Indicator	pH range
A	Methyl orange	4·2 – 6·3
B	Bromothymol blue	6·0 – 7·6
C	Phenol red	6·8 – 8·4
D	Phenolphthalein	8·3 – 10·0

15. The standard enthalpy of formation of magnesium bromide is the enthalpy change for the reaction

    A $Mg^{2+}(g) + 2Br^-(g) \rightarrow Mg^{2+}(Br^-)_2(s)$

    B $Mg^{2+}(g) + 2Br^-(g) \rightarrow Mg^{2+}(Br^-)_2(g)$

    C $Mg(s) + Br_2(g) \rightarrow Mg^{2+}(Br^-)_2(s)$

    D $Mg(s) + Br_2(\ell) \rightarrow Mg^{2+}(Br^-)_2(s)$.

16. The standard enthalpy of combustion of hydrogen is -286 kJ mol^{-1}.

    The standard enthalpy of formation of water, in kJ mol^{-1}, is

    A -286

    B -143

    C $+143$

    D $+286$.

17. Which of the following enthalpy changes can be measured directly by experiment?

    A   Bond enthalpy of C–H bond

    B   Enthalpy of formation of ethane

    C   Lattice enthalpy of magnesium oxide

    D   Enthalpy of solution of potassium chloride

18. In which of the following does X represent the bond enthalpy for the O–H bond in water?

    A $H_2O(g) \rightarrow O(g) + H_2(g)$ $\Delta H = 2X$

    B $H_2O(g) \rightarrow O(g) + 2H(g)$ $\Delta H = 2X$

    C $H_2O(g) \rightarrow O(g) + H_2(g)$ $\Delta H = X$

    D $H_2O(g) \rightarrow O(g) + 2H(g)$ $\Delta H = X$

19. The enthalpy change for

    $Li^+(g) + Br^-(g) \rightarrow Li^+(aq) + Br^-(aq)$

    is

    A   the enthalpy of formation of lithium bromide

    B   the enthalpy of solution of lithium bromide

    C   the sum of the hydration enthalpies of lithium and bromide ions

    D   the sum of the first ionisation energy of lithium and the electron affinity of bromine.

Questions **20** and **21** refer to the Born-Haber cycle below.

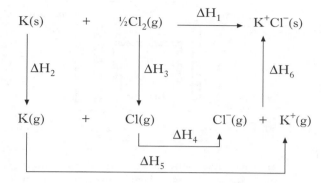

20. The enthalpy change which requires the input of most energy is

    A ΔH_2

    B ΔH_3

    C ΔH_4

    D ΔH_5.

21. The main enthalpy term which ensures that ΔH_1 is exothermic is

    A ΔH_3

    B ΔH_4

    C ΔH_5

    D ΔH_6.

22. Which line in the table shows the correct signs of ΔG° and E° for a feasible reaction occurring under standard conditions?

	ΔG°	E°
A	+	+
B	+	−
C	−	+
D	−	−

23. For the following cell

    $Ni(s) \mid Ni^{2+}(aq) \parallel Cu^{2+}(aq) \mid Cu(s)$

    the species being reduced is

    A $Ni(s)$

    B $Ni^{2+}(aq)$

    C $Cu^{2+}(aq)$

    D $Cu(s)$.

24.

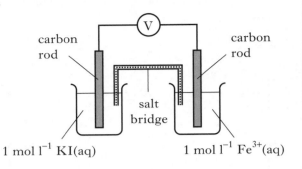

1 mol l^{-1} KI(aq)   1 mol l^{-1} Fe^{3+}(aq)

In the electrochemical cell shown above, operating under standard conditions, the emf produced would be

A   0·23 V

B   0·58 V

C   1·00 V

D   2·88 V.

25. $C_3H_7Cl + C_2H_5O^- \rightarrow C_3H_7OC_2H_5 + Cl^-$

The above reaction is

A   an elimination reaction

B   a nucleophilic addition reaction

C   a nucleophilic substitution reaction

D   an electrophilic substitution reaction.

26. Which of the following does **not** occur in the reaction between methane and chlorine?

A   A chain reaction

B   Homolytic fission

C   Free radical formation

D   An addition reaction

27. Which of the following compounds is likely to be the most soluble in water?

A

H H H H
| | | |
H — C — C — C — C — C — H
| | ‖ | |
H H O H H

B

H H H H   O
| | | | ‖
H — C — C — C — C — C
| | | | \
H H H H   H

C

H H H H   O
| | | | ‖
H — C — C — C — C — C
| | | | \
H H H H   OH

D

H H H H H   O
| | | | | ‖
H — C — C — C — C — C — C
| | | | | \
H H H H H   OH

28. The sideways overlap of two parallel atomic orbitals lying perpendicular to the axis of the bond is known as

A   hybridisation

B   a pi bond

C   a sigma bond

D   a double bond.

29. If the structure of 3-methylcyclobutene can be represented by

then the structure of 1-ethyl-3-methylcyclopentene will be represented by

A

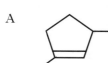

B

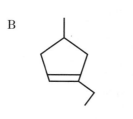

C

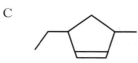

D

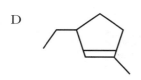

30. Caryophyllene ($C_{15}H_{24}$) is an unsaturated cyclic hydrocarbon.

Complete hydrogenation of caryophyllene gives a saturated hydrocarbon $C_{15}H_{28}$.

Which line in the table shows the correct numbers of double bonds and rings in caryophyllene?

	Number of double bonds	Number of rings
A	2	1
B	2	2
C	4	2
D	4	4

31. Which of the following is most reactive as a nucleophile?

A Br_2

B CH_3I

C NH_4^+

D NH_3

32. Hydrogen bonding occurs in

A CH_3I

B CH_3OH

C CH_3OCH_3

D $CH_3CH_2CHO.$

33. Cinnamaldehyde, which can be extracted from cinnamon, has the structure:

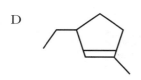

Cinnamaldehyde will **not** react with

A sodium metal

B bromine solution

C lithium aluminium hydride

D acidified potassium dichromate.

34. Which of the following compounds would be produced by passing ammonia gas into dilute ethanoic acid?

A CH_3CONH_2

B $CH_3COO^-NH_4^+$

C NH_2CH_2COOH

D $CH_3CH_2NH_3^+Cl^-$

[Turn over

35. Secondary amines react with carbonyl compounds to form unsaturated amines known as enamines as shown

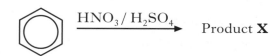

an enamine

Which carbonyl compound would react with $(CH_3)_2NH$ to form the enamine with the following structure?

A   Propanal

B   Propanone

C   Butanal

D   Butanone

36.

$$\underset{}{\bigcirc} \xrightarrow{HNO_3 / H_2SO_4} \text{Product } \mathbf{X}$$

Which line in the table is correct for the reaction above?

	Type of reaction	Product **X**
A	electrophilic substitution	benzene ring with NO₂
B	electrophilic substitution	benzene ring with SO₃H
C	nucleophilic substitution	benzene ring with NO₂
D	nucleophilic substitution	benzene ring with SO₃H

37. Which of the following statements about the benzene molecule is **not** true?

A   It is planar.

B   It has empirical formula CH.

C   It is readily attacked by bromine.

D   Its C—C bonds are equal in length.

38. Which of the following could **not** exist in isomeric forms?

A C_3H_6

B C_3H_8

C C_3H_7Br

D $C_2H_4Cl_2$

39. Which of the following causes the separation of the ions in a mass spectrometer?

A   A magnetic field

B   A vacuum pump

C   An ionisation chamber

D   Electron bombardment

40. Which of the following compounds is most likely to show an infra-red absorption at 2725 cm^{-1}?

A $CH_3 - \underset{\underset{O}{\|}}{C} - CH_3$

B $HOCH_2CH = CH_2$

C $CH_3 - CH_2 - C\overset{\displaystyle O}{\underset{\displaystyle H}{<}}$

D $CH_3 - O - CH = CH_2$

SECTION B

60 marks are available in this section of the paper.

All answers must be written clearly and legibly in ink.

Marks

1. The first argon compound was prepared by shining light of wavelength 160 nm onto a mixture of argon and hydrogen fluoride at a temperature of 7·5 K. The hydrogen fluoride reacted with the argon to form HArF.

   (a) Calculate the energy, in kJ mol^{-1}, associated with light of wavelength 160 nm.   **2**

   (b) Supposing HArF is covalent,

       (i) predict the total number of electron pairs, bonding and non-bonding, which surround the Ar atom in the HArF molecule.   **1**

       (ii) what shape do the electron pairs around the Ar atom in an HArF molecule adopt?   **1**

           (4)

2. Complex ions **A** and **B** are isomeric and have the formula $[Cr(H_2O)_4Cl_2]^+$.

   (a) Calculate the oxidation number of chromium in the complex ion.   **1**

   (b) Name the complex ion.   **1**

   (c) The structural formula for complex ion **A** is

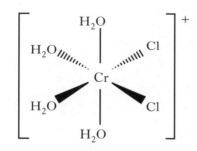

   Draw the structural formula for complex ion **B**.   **1**

           (3)

[Turn over

Marks

3. The Thermit process can be used to extract iron from iron(III) oxide.

$$2Al(s) + Fe_2O_3(s) \rightarrow 2Fe(s) + Al_2O_3(s)$$

Substance	Standard enthalpy of formation, $\Delta H°/kJ\ mol^{-1}$	Standard entropy, $S°/J\ K^{-1}\ mol^{-1}$
Al(s)	0	28·0
$Fe_2O_3(s)$	-824	87·0
Fe(s)	0	27·0
$Al_2O_3(s)$	-1676	51·0

For the Thermit process, use the data in the table to calculate

(*a*) the standard enthalpy change, $\Delta H°$ 1

(*b*) the standard entropy change, $\Delta S°$ 1

(*c*) the standard free energy change, $\Delta G°$.   2

(4)

Marks

4. In a PPA, a sample of steel was treated in a sequence of reactions to determine the manganese content.

The absorbance of a sample of the permanganate solution formed was analysed using a colorimeter fitted with a 520 nm filter. Optically matched cuvettes were used throughout.

(a) (i) Apart from the steel dissolving in the hot nitric acid, what would have been observed at step one?   **1**

    (ii) In step two, Mn^{2+}(aq) is converted into MnO_4^-(aq). What is the role of the potassium periodate, KIO_4?   **1**

    (iii) Why was a 520 nm filter used?   **1**

(b) A series of standard permanganate solutions were used to produce the calibration graph below.

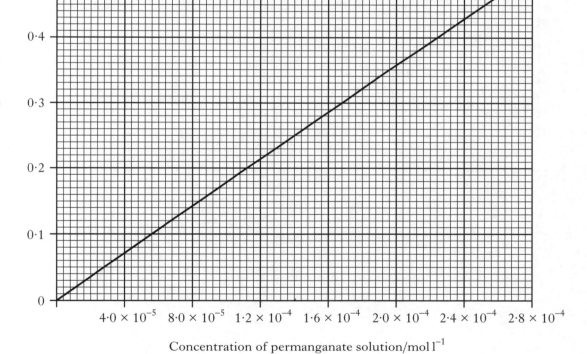

Concentration of permanganate solution/mol l^{-1}

The results of the experiment are shown below.

Mass of steel used	=	0·19 g
Absorbance of permanganate solution	=	0·25
Total volume of permanganate solution	=	100 cm^3

Use the graph and the results to calculate the percentage, by mass, of manganese in the sample of steel.   **3**

(6)

Marks

5. The nitrate ion has three equivalent resonance structures. One of these structures is shown below.

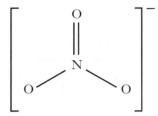

(a) Draw a similar diagram to show one of the other two resonance structures. **1**

(b) The formal charge on an atom in a resonance structure can be found using the expression

$$\text{Formal charge} = \left(\begin{array}{c}\text{Group in}\\\text{Periodic Table}\end{array}\right) - \left(\begin{array}{c}\text{Number of lone pair}\\\text{electrons}\end{array}\right) - \tfrac{1}{2}\left(\begin{array}{c}\text{Number of bonding}\\\text{electrons}\end{array}\right).$$

Use this expression to find the formal charge on atoms (b), (c) and (d) shown in the table below.

Resonance structure	Atom	Formal charge
	(a)	+1
	(b)	?
	(c)	?
	(d)	?

2

(3)

Marks

6. The formula of potassium hydrogen oxalate can be written as $K_xH_y(C_2O_4)_z$.

   In an experiment to determine the values of **x, y** and **z**, 4·49 g of this compound was dissolved in water and the solution made up to one litre.

   (a) 20·0 cm³ of the solution was pipetted into a conical flask and then titrated with 0·0200 mol l⁻¹ acidified potassium permanganate at 60 °C. The average titre volume was 16·5 cm³.

   The equation for the reaction taking place in the conical flask is

   $$5C_2O_4^{2-} + 16H^+ + 2MnO_4^- \rightarrow 2Mn^{2+} + 10CO_2 + 8H_2O$$

   (i) What colour change would indicate the end point of the titration?   1

   (ii) From the titration result, calculate the number of moles of oxalate ions, $C_2O_4^{2-}$, in 20·0 cm³ of the solution.   1

   (iii) Calculate the mass of oxalate ions in one litre of the solution.   1

   (iv) Using another analytical procedure, 4·49 g of potassium hydrogen oxalate was found to contain 0·060 g of hydrogen.

   Use this information with the answer to (a)(iii) to calculate the mass of potassium in this sample.   1

   (b) Calculate the values of **x, y** and **z**.   2

   (6)

7. The expression for the equilibrium constant of an esterification reaction is

   $$K = \frac{[CH_3COOCH_2CH_3]\,[H_2O]}{[CH_3COOH]\,[CH_3CH_2OH]}$$

   (a) Write the chemical equation for this esterification reaction.   1

   (b) In an experiment to determine the value of the equilibrium constant, 0·70 moles of ethanoic acid and 0·68 moles of ethanol were mixed in a conical flask. The flask was stoppered to prevent the contents escaping and then placed in a water bath at 50 °C.

   At equilibrium the mixture contained 0·24 moles of ethanoic acid.

   (i) Why is it important to prevent the contents of the flask escaping?   1

   (ii) Calculate K at 50 °C.   3

   (5)

8. Nicotinic acid is used in the treatment of high cholesterol levels. A structural formula for nicotinic acid is

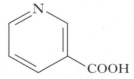

   (a) Write an equation to show the dissociation of nicotinic acid in water.   1

   (b) The K_a value of nicotinic acid is $1\cdot4 \times 10^{-5}$.

   Calculate the concentration of a nicotinic acid solution which has a pH of 3·77.   3

   (4)

Marks

9. The rate equation for the reaction between nitrogen dioxide and fluorine is

$$Rate = k[NO_2][F_2]$$

A proposed reaction mechanism is

Step one $NO_2 + F_2 \rightarrow NO_2F + F$

Step two $NO_2 + F \rightarrow NO_2F.$

(a) Which step in the proposed reaction mechanism would be **faster**?   1

(b) Write a balanced equation for the overall reaction.   1

(c) What is the overall order of the reaction?   1

(d)

Experiment	$[NO_2]/mol\ l^{-1}$	$[F_2]/mol\ l^{-1}$	Initial rate/ $mol\ l^{-1}\ s^{-1}$
1	0·001	0·003	$1·2 \times 10^{-4}$
2	0·006	0·001	$2·4 \times 10^{-4}$
3	0·002	0·004	$3·2 \times 10^{-4}$

Use the data in the table to calculate a value for the rate constant, k, including the appropriate units.   2

(5)

10. Alkenes can be prepared from alcohols.

In a PPA, 22·56 g of cyclohexanol was dehydrated using an excess of concentrated phosphoric acid. The reaction mixture was then distilled. The crude cyclohexene was added to a separating funnel containing a solution which was used to wash the cyclohexene and improve the separation of the aqueous and organic layers. The organic layer was separated and treated with anhydrous calcium chloride before it was distilled to yield 6·52 g of pure cyclohexene.

(a) Why was concentrated phosphoric acid used as the dehydrating agent rather than concentrated sulphuric acid?   1

(b) Name the solution that the crude cyclohexene was added to in the separating funnel.   1

(c) What was the function of the anhydrous calcium chloride?   1

(d) The relative formula masses of cyclohexanol and cyclohexene are 100 and 82 respectively.

Calculate the percentage yield of cyclohexene.   2

(5)

Marks

11. Consider the following reaction scheme.

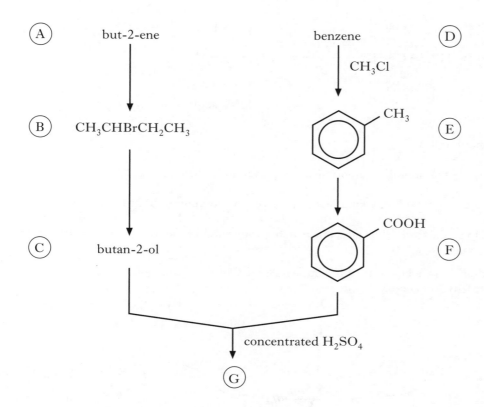

(a) Explain why but-2-ene exhibits geometric isomerism yet its structural isomer but-1-ene does not. 1

(b) But-2-ene undergoes electrophilic addition to form (B).

Draw a structure for the carbocation intermediate formed in this electrophilic addition reaction. 1

(c) Name a reagent used to convert (B) to (C). 1

(d) Name a catalyst required in converting (D) to (E). 1

(e) Draw a structural formula for ester (G). 1

(5)

[Turn over

Marks

12. Consider the following reaction sequence.

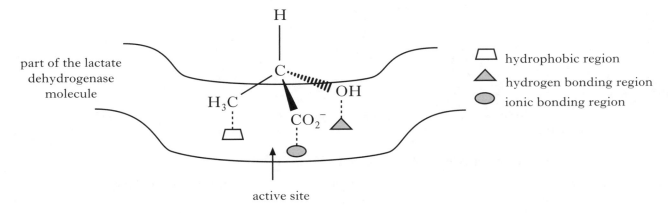

(a) Name compound **A**. 1

(b) To which class of organic compounds does compound **B** belong? 1

(c) Name the type of reaction taking place in converting compound **B** into lactic acid. 1

(d) Lactic acid in the form of lactate ions is dehydrogenated in the liver by the enzyme, lactate dehydrogenase.

The diagram shows how one of the optical isomers of the lactate ion binds to an active site of lactate dehydrogenase.

(i) Which type of intermolecular force is involved when the methyl group of the lactate ion binds to the hydrophobic region of the active site? 1

(ii) Draw a structure for the other optical isomer of the lactate ion. 1

(iii) Explain why this other optical isomer of the lactate ion cannot bind as efficiently to the active site of lactate dehydrogenase. 1

(6)

Marks

13. Compound **A** has molecular formula $C_4H_{10}O$.

    (*a*) To which two classes of organic compounds could **A** belong?

    2

    (*b*) Compound **A** reacts with acidified potassium dichromate solution to form **B** which has molecular formula C_4H_8O.

    The proton nmr spectrum of **B** shows three peaks. Analysis of this spectrum produces the following data.

Peak	Chemical shift/ppm	Relative area under peak
1	0·95	3
2	2·05	3
3	2·35	2

    Considering all the evidence above:

    (i) draw a structural formula for **B**;

    1

    (ii) name **A**.

    1

    (4)

[*END OF QUESTION PAPER*]

[BLANK PAGE]

ADVANCED HIGHER

2011

[BLANK PAGE]

X012/701

NATIONAL
QUALIFICATIONS
2011

THURSDAY, 26 MAY
9.00 AM – 11.30 AM

CHEMISTRY
ADVANCED HIGHER

Reference may be made to the Chemistry Higher and Advanced Higher Data Booklet .

SECTION A – 40 marks

Instructions for completion of **SECTION A** are given on page two.

For this section of the examination you must use an **HB pencil**.

SECTION B – 60 marks

All questions should be attempted.

Answers must be written clearly and legibly in ink.

SECTION A

Read carefully

1 Check that the answer sheet provided is for **Chemistry Advanced Higher (Section A)**.

2 For this section of the examination you must use an **HB pencil** and, where necessary, an eraser.

3 Check that the answer sheet you have been given has **your name**, **date of birth**, **SCN** (Scottish Candidate Number) and **Centre Name** printed on it.

Do not change any of these details.

4 If any of this information is wrong, tell the Invigilator immediately.

5 If this information is correct, **print** your name and seat number in the boxes provided.

6 The answer to each question is **either** A, B, C or D. Decide what your answer is, then, using your pencil, put a horizontal line in the space provided (see sample question below).

7 There is **only one correct** answer to each question.

8 Any rough working should be done on the question paper or the rough working sheet, **not** on your answer sheet.

9 At the end of the exam, put the **answer sheet for Section A inside the front cover of your answer book**.

Sample Question

To show that the ink in a ball-pen consists of a mixture of dyes, the method of separation would be

        A chromatography

        B fractional distillation

        C fractional crystallisation

        D filtration.

The correct answer is **A**—chromatography. The answer **A** has been clearly marked in **pencil** with a horizontal line (see below).

Changing an answer

If you decide to change your answer, carefully erase your first answer and using your pencil, fill in the answer you want. The answer below has been changed to **D**.

1. Which of the following lines on the graph represents the trend in successive ionisation energies of a Group 3 element?

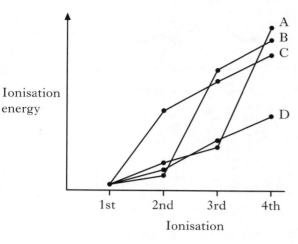

2. In colorimetry, as the concentration of a coloured solution decreases

   A   the absorbance increases

   B   the absorbance decreases

   C   the radiation wavelength increases

   D   the radiation wavelength decreases.

3. Which of the following molecules has the greatest number of non-bonding electron pairs (lone pairs)?

   A $H-\overset{\displaystyle H}{\underset{\displaystyle H}{C}}-Cl$

   B $H-\overset{\displaystyle H}{\underset{\displaystyle H}{C}}-O-H$

   C $H-\overset{\displaystyle H}{\underset{\displaystyle H}{C}}-N\big<{}^{H}_{H}$

   D $H-\overset{\displaystyle H}{C}=O$

4. What is the change in the three-dimensional arrangement of the bonds round the P atom in the following reaction?

$$PF_5 \rightarrow PF_3 + F_2$$

   A   Tetrahedral to pyramidal

   B   Octahedral to trigonal planar

   C   Trigonal bipyramidal to pyramidal

   D   Trigonal bipyramidal to trigonal planar

5. The ratio of the ionic radii in sodium chloride is approximately 1:2, whereas in caesium chloride it is approximately 1:1. A compound XY contains X^+ ions with a radius of 133 pm and Y^- ions with a radius of 220 pm.

In a crystal of XY, how many Y^- ions surround each X^+ ion as its nearest neighbour?

   A   1

   B   2

   C   6

   D   8

6. An example of a p-type semiconductor is silicon doped with

   A   carbon

   B   arsenic

   C   aluminium

   D   phosphorus.

7. Which of the following solid oxides would **not** lower the pH when added to sodium hydroxide solution?

   A Li_2O

   B SiO_2

   C P_4O_{10}

   D Al_2O_3

[Turn over

8. Which of the following is least likely to produce fumes of hydrogen chloride when added to water?

   A PCl_5

   B $SiCl_4$

   C $AlCl_3$

   D $MgCl_2$

9. A white solid gives an orange-yellow flame colour. When added to water, hydrogen gas is released and an alkaline solution is formed.

   The solid could be

   A   sodium oxide

   B   calcium oxide

   C   sodium hydride

   D   calcium hydride.

10. Which of the following ions is **least** likely to be coloured?

   A $Ti(H_2O)_6^{3+}$

   B $Cr(NH_3)_6^{3+}$

   C $Ni(H_2O)_6^{2+}$

   D $Zn(NH_3)_4^{2+}$

11. What volume of $0.25\,mol\,l^{-1}$ calcium nitrate is required to make, by dilution with water, $500\,cm^3$ of a solution with a **nitrate** ion concentration of $0.1\,mol\,l^{-1}$?

   A $50\,cm^3$

   B $100\,cm^3$

   C $200\,cm^3$

   D $400\,cm^3$

12. Hydrogen for use in ammonia production is produced by the endothermic reaction:

   $$CH_4(g) + H_2O(g) \rightleftharpoons CO(g) + 3H_2(g)$$

   Which of the following will increase the equilibrium yield of hydrogen?

   A   Decrease the methane concentration

   B   Decrease the temperature

   C   Decrease the pressure

   D   Add a catalyst

13. The reaction

   $$CO(g) + 3H_2(g) \rightleftharpoons CH_4(g) + H_2O(g)$$

   has an equilibrium constant of 3.9 at $950\,^\circ C$.

   The equilibrium concentrations of $CO(g)$, $H_2(g)$ and $H_2O(g)$ are given in the table.

Substance	Equilibrium concentration/$mol\,l^{-1}$
$CO(g)$	0·500
$H_2(g)$	0·100
$H_2O(g)$	0·040

   What is the equilibrium concentration of $CH_4(g)$, in $mol\,l^{-1}$, at $950\,^\circ C$?

   A   0·049

   B   0·200

   C   4·90

   D   20·0

14.

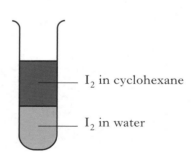

   The partition coefficient for the above system can be altered by

   A   adding more iodine

   B   adding more cyclohexane

   C   changing the temperature

   D   shaking the mixture thoroughly.

15. Gas liquid chromatography could be used to separate a mixture of hydrocarbons. The mixture is passed through a column packed with silica particles coated in a non-polar liquid. Helium can be used to carry the mixture through the column.

Which line in the table identifies correctly the stationary and mobile phases in this chromatographic separation?

	Stationary phase	Mobile phase
A	silica	helium
B	silica	non-polar liquid
C	non-polar liquid	helium
D	non-polar liquid	hydrocarbon mixture

16. Under certain conditions liquid ammonia ionises as shown:

$$2NH_3 \rightleftharpoons NH_4^+ + NH_2^-$$

Which line in the table shows the correct conjugate acid and conjugate base for this ionisation?

	Conjugate acid	Conjugate base
A	NH_3	NH_4^+
B	NH_4^+	NH_3
C	NH_2^-	NH_4^+
D	NH_4^+	NH_2^-

17. The activation energies for the reactions

   (1) $H_2(g) + I_2(g) \rightarrow 2HI(g)$

   (2) $2HI(g) \rightarrow H_2(g) + I_2(g)$

are 165 kJ and 179 kJ respectively. The enthalpy change for reaction (2) is

A -14 kJ

B $+14$ kJ

C -344 kJ

D $+344$ kJ.

18. The standard enthalpy of formation of strontium chloride is the enthalpy change for which of the following reactions?

A $Sr(g) + Cl_2(g) \rightarrow SrCl_2(s)$

B $Sr(s) + Cl_2(g) \rightarrow SrCl_2(s)$

C $Sr^{2+}(g) + 2Cl^-(g) \rightarrow SrCl_2(s)$

D $Sr^{2+}(aq) + 2Cl^-(aq) \rightarrow SrCl_2(s)$

19. Consider the following thermochemical cycle which is not drawn to scale.

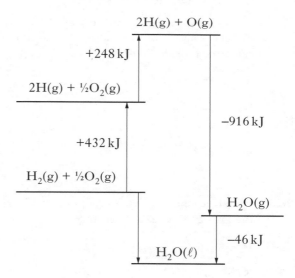

The enthalpy change for the reaction

$2H_2(g) + O_2(g) \rightarrow 2H_2O(\ell)$ is

A -564 kJ

B -282 kJ

C $+564$ kJ

D $+1642$ kJ.

20. In the presence of bright light, hydrogen and chlorine react explosively. One step in the reaction is shown below.

$$H_2(g) + Cl(g) \rightarrow HCl(g) + H(g)$$

The enthalpy change for this step can be represented as the bond enthalpy of

   A   (H—H) + (Cl—Cl)

   B   (H—H) – (Cl—Cl)

   C   (H—H) + (H—Cl)

   D   (H—H) – (H—Cl).

21. The standard enthalpy of atomisation of bromine is the enthalpy change for the reaction

   A $\frac{1}{2}Br_2(s) \rightarrow Br(g)$

   B $\frac{1}{2}Br_2(\ell) \rightarrow Br(g)$

   C $\frac{1}{2}Br_2(g) \rightarrow Br(g)$

   D $Br_2(g) \rightarrow 2Br(g)$.

22. The enthalpy of solution of a compound can be calculated from its lattice enthalpy and the hydration enthalpies of its ions.

Using information from the Data Booklet, the correct value for enthalpy of solution of calcium chloride, in $kJ\,mol^{-1}$, is

   A   −155

   B   +155

   C   −209

   D   +209.

23. Which of the following reactions would show the greatest decrease in entropy?

A $H_2(g) + F_2(g) \rightarrow 2HF(g)$

B $KNO_3(s) \rightarrow KNO_2(s) + \frac{1}{2}O_2(g)$

C $CO_3^{2-}(aq) + 2H^+(aq) \rightarrow H_2O(\ell) + CO_2(g)$

D $CO_3^{2-}(aq) + CO_2(g) + H_2O(\ell) \rightarrow 2HCO_3^-(aq)$

24. Which of the following alcohols would have the greatest entropy at 90 °C?

   A   Propan-1-ol

   B   Propan-2-ol

   C   Butan-1-ol

   D   Butan-2-ol

25. Which of the following redox equations represents a reaction which is not feasible under standard conditions?

   A $F_2(g) + 2Cl^-(aq) \rightarrow 2F^-(aq) + Cl_2(g)$

   B $Cl_2(g) + 2Br^-(aq) \rightarrow 2Cl^-(aq) + Br_2(\ell)$

   C $F_2(g) + 2Br^-(aq) \rightarrow 2F^-(aq) + Br_2(\ell)$

   D $I_2(s) + 2Br^-(aq) \rightarrow 2I^-(aq) + Br_2(\ell)$

26. Propene can be produced by heating 1-bromopropane with ethanolic potassium hydroxide.

This reaction is an example of

   A   reduction

   B   hydrolysis

   C   elimination

   D   condensation.

27. The structures of three alcohols, **P**, **Q**, and **R** are shown.

P
$$H-\underset{\underset{H}{|}}{\overset{\overset{H}{|}}{C}}-\underset{\underset{H}{|}}{\overset{\overset{H}{|}}{C}}-\underset{\underset{H}{|}}{\overset{\overset{OH}{|}}{C}}-H$$

Q
$$H-\underset{\underset{H}{|}}{\overset{\overset{H}{|}}{C}}-\underset{\underset{H}{|}}{\overset{\overset{OH}{|}}{C}}-\underset{\underset{H}{|}}{\overset{\overset{OH}{|}}{C}}-H$$

R
$$H-\underset{\underset{H}{|}}{\overset{\overset{OH}{|}}{C}}-\underset{\underset{H}{|}}{\overset{\overset{OH}{|}}{C}}-\underset{\underset{H}{|}}{\overset{\overset{OH}{|}}{C}}-H$$

Which line in the table describes correctly the trends in boiling points and viscosities on moving from **P** to **Q** to **R**?

	Boiling point	Viscosity
A	increases	increases
B	increases	decreases
C	decreases	increases
D	decreases	decreases

28. Which of the following best describes the bonding in ethane?

A sp^2 hybridisation of the carbon atoms giving sigma bonds only

B sp^2 hybridisation of the carbon atoms giving sigma and pi bonds

C sp^3 hybridisation of the carbon atoms giving sigma bonds only

D sp^3 hybridisation of the carbon atoms giving sigma and pi bonds

29. Part of a possible chain reaction mechanism for chlorine reacting with methane is:

$$Cl_2 \rightarrow 2Cl\bullet$$
$$Cl\bullet + CH_4 \rightarrow HCl + CH_3\bullet$$
$$CH_3\bullet + Cl_2 \rightarrow CH_3Cl + Cl\bullet$$

Which of the following will **not** be a termination step in this reaction?

A $H\bullet + Cl\bullet \rightarrow HCl$

B $Cl\bullet + Cl\bullet \rightarrow Cl_2$

C $CH_3\bullet + CH_3\bullet \rightarrow C_2H_6$

D $CH_3\bullet + Cl\bullet \rightarrow CH_3Cl$

30. Pyridine, C_5H_5N, has the following structure:

Which line in the table shows the correct numbers of σ and π bonds in a molecule of pyridine?

	Number of σ bonds	Number of π bonds
A	3	11
B	6	3
C	11	3
D	12	3

31. The major product in the reaction of HCl with 2-methylpent-2-ene,

$$H_3C-\underset{\overset{|}{\overset{CH_3}{}}}{C}=CH-CH_2-CH_3 \text{ is}$$

A 2-chloro-2-methylpentane

B 3-chloro-2-methylpentane

C 2,3-dichloro-2-methylpentane

D 4-chloro-4-methylpentane.

[Turn over

32. A compound, **X**, reacts with the product of its own oxidation to form an ester.

    X could be

    A   propanal

    B   propan-1-ol

    C   propan-2-ol

    D   propanoic acid.

33. Which of the following amines does **not** have hydrogen bonds between its molecules in the liquid state?

    A $CH_3CH_2CH_2CH_2NH_2$

    B $CH_3CH_2NHCH_2CH_3$

    C $(CH_3)_2CHCH_2NH_2$

    D $(CH_3)_2NCH_2CH_3$

34. 1 mole of which of the following compounds would react with the largest volume of $1\ mol\,l^{-1}$ hydrochloric acid?

    A CH_3NHCH_3

    B $H_2NCH_2NH_2$

    C $CH_2OHCHOHCH_2OH$

    D   HO—⬡—NH_2

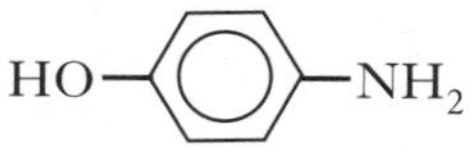

35. The conversion of benzene to monochlorobenzene using $Cl_2/FeCl_3$ involves

    A   nucleophilic addition

    B   nucleophilic substitution

    C   electrophilic addition

    D   electrophilic substitution.

36.

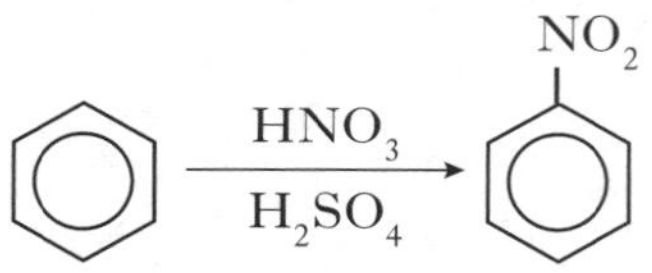

    Which species initially attacks the benzene molecule in the above reaction?

    A NO_3^-

    B NO_2^+

    C HSO_4^-

    D NO_2

37. Which of the following is the geometric isomer of *trans*-1,2-dibromopropene?

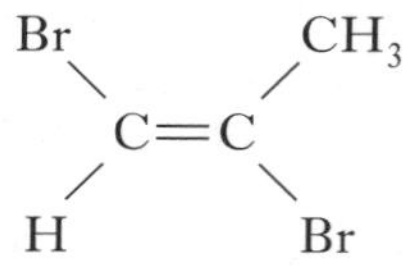

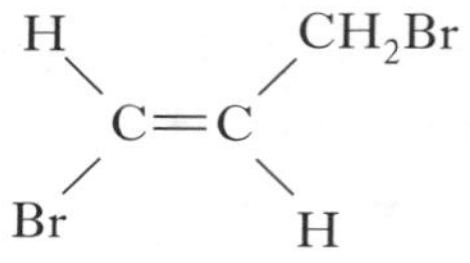

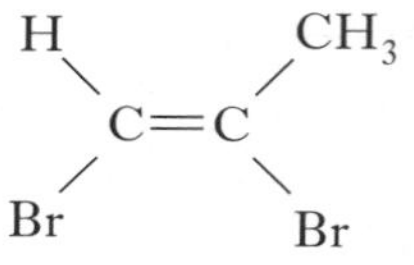

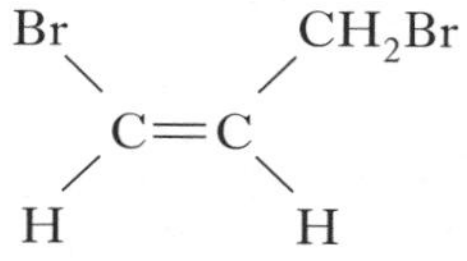

38. The mass spectrum of an organic compound, empirical formula C_2H_4O, shows a peak for the parent ion at mass/charge ratio of 88.

    The organic compound could **not** be

    A   ethanal

    B   butanoic acid

    C   ethyl ethanoate

    D   methyl propanoate.

39. From which region of the electromagnetic spectrum is energy absorbed in the production of proton nmr spectra?

A   X-rays

B   Visible

C   Infra-red

D   Radio waves

40. A compound, which has molecular formula C_4H_8O, has only 2 peaks in its low resolution proton nmr spectrum.

A possible structural formula for this compound is

A $CH_3CH_2CCH_3$
                $\|$
                O

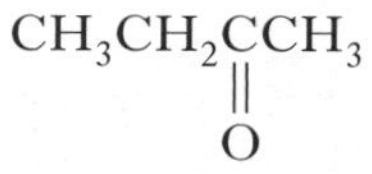

B $CH_3CH_2CH_2CHO$

C $CH_3-\overset{\overset{\displaystyle CH_3}{|}}{\underset{\underset{\displaystyle OH}{|}}{C}}-CH_3$

D $\begin{array}{c} H_2C-CH_2 \\ \diagup \qquad \diagdown \\ H_2C \qquad CH_2 \\ \diagdown \quad \diagup \\ O \end{array}$

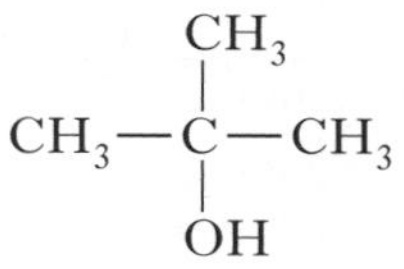

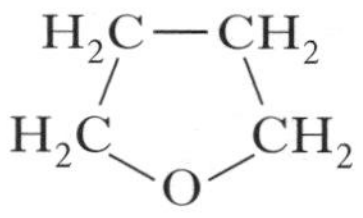

[END OF SECTION A]

Candidates are reminded that the answer sheet for Section A MUST be placed INSIDE the front cover of your answer book.

[Turn over for SECTION B on *Page ten*

SECTION B

Marks

60 marks are available in this section of the paper.

All answers must be written clearly and legibly in ink.

1. The compound, $Sn_2Ba_2(Sr_{0.5}Y_{0.5})Cu_3O_8$, has zero electrical resistance at 85 K.

    (a) What name is given to this phenomenon?   **1**

    (b) Which liquid coolant can be used economically and safely at this temperature?   **1**

                                                                                                    (2)

2. When hydrogen is subjected to a high voltage in a gas discharge tube and the emitted light is passed through a prism the atomic emission spectrum produced is as shown below.

    hydrogen emission spectrum (visible region)

    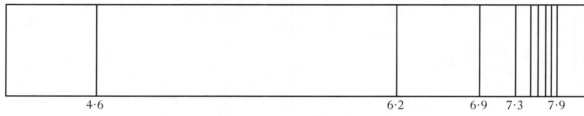

    Frequency $\nu/10^{14}$ Hz

    (a) Which line in the spectrum is red?   **1**

    (b) The ionisation energy of hydrogen has a value of 1311 kJ mol^{-1}.

        (i) Write the equation for the ionisation energy of hydrogen.   **1**

        (ii) Calculate the wavelength of the light corresponding to this ionisation energy.   **3**

                                                                                                    (5)

Marks

3. When a mixture of nitrogen monoxide and nitrogen dioxide is cooled to −20 °C they react to form the clear blue liquid, dinitrogen trioxide.

$$NO + NO_2 \rightarrow N_2O_3$$

(a) The oxidation state of nitrogen is **different** in each of these three compounds.

Calculate the oxidation states of the nitrogen in NO and NO_2 respectively.

1

(b) Dinitrogen trioxide neutralises aqueous sodium hydroxide forming sodium nitrite and water.

The nitrite ion, NO_2^-, can be represented by two resonance structures.

One of these is

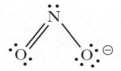

Draw the other resonance structure.

1

(c) In aqueous solution the nitrite ion can be oxidised to the nitrate ion.

Write the ion-electron equation for this oxidation.

1

(3)

[Turn over

Marks

4. Iron and manganese are transition metals which have many uses in industry.

    The electronic configuration for iron, in its ground state, is

    $$1s^2 2s^2 2p^6 3s^2 3p^6 3d^6 4s^2$$

    (a) In terms of s, p and d orbitals write down the electronic configurations of

         (i) Fe^{3+}

         (ii) Mn^{3+}

         in their ground states.   2

         (iii) Explain why the Fe^{3+} ion is more stable than the Mn^{3+} ion.   1

    (b) The transition metal titanium is the seventh most abundant element in the Earth's crust.

         Two of the reactions involved in the conversion of the ore ilmenite, $FeTiO_3$, into metallic titanium are shown below.

         Step 1—Ilmenite is reacted with concentrated sulphuric acid.

         $$FeTiO_3(s) + 3H_2SO_4(\ell) \rightarrow FeSO_4(aq) + Ti(SO_4)_2(aq) + 3H_2O(\ell)$$

         Step 2—After separation the titanium sulphate is reacted with sodium hydroxide.

         $$Ti(SO_4)_2(aq) + 4NaOH(aq) \rightarrow TiO_2(s) + 2H_2O(\ell) + 2Na_2SO_4(aq)$$

         How many kilograms of titanium oxide can theoretically be produced from 3·25 kg of ilmenite?   2

    (c) Transition metals can form a wide variety of complexes. One such complex is ammonium tetrachlorocuprate(II).

         Write the formula for this complex.   1

                                                                                         (6)

Marks

5.   The PPA "Complexometric Determination of Nickel using EDTA" has two main stages.

      Stage 1   Preparation of nickel(II) sulphate solution.

      Stage 2   Titration of the nickel(II) sulphate solution with EDTA.

The instructions for **Stage 1** are shown below.

1.   Accurately weigh out approximately $2 \cdot 6\,g$ of hydrated nickel(II) sulphate, $NiSO_4.6H_2O$.

2.   Transfer the hydrated nickel salt to a $100\,cm^3$ beaker, add $25\,cm^3$ of deionised water and stir to dissolve the solid.

3.   Transfer the solution to a $100\,cm^3$ standard flask.

4.

5.

6.   Stopper the flask and invert it several times to ensure the contents are thoroughly mixed.

(*a*)   Complete the instructions for steps 4 and 5.   **1**

(*b*)   In **Stage 2**, $25 \cdot 0\,cm^3$ of the nickel(II) sulphate solution were titrated against $0 \cdot 110\,mol\,l^{-1}$ EDTA solution.

The results of the titrations are shown below

	Rough titre	1st titre	2nd titre
Initial burette reading/cm^3	2·00	25·90	10·00
Final burette reading/cm^3	25·90	49·40	33·60
Volume of EDTA added/cm^3	23·90	23·50	23·60

The equation for the reaction is represented by

$$Ni^{2+}(aq) + [EDTA]^{4-}(aq) \longrightarrow Ni[EDTA]^{2-}(aq)$$

   (i)   Name the indicator used to detect the end-point of the titration in this PPA.   **1**

  (ii)   EDTA acts as a hexadentate ligand. What shape is the complex ion $Ni[EDTA]^{2-}$?   **1**

 (iii)   The accurate mass of the nickel(II) sulphate used was $2 \cdot 656\,g$.

      Calculate the percentage by mass of nickel present in the hydrated salt from these experimental results.   **3**

(6)

[Turn over

Marks

6. The standard free energy change for a chemical reaction is given by the expression

$$\Delta G^\circ = \Delta H^\circ - T\Delta S^\circ$$

The expression can be rearranged to give

$$\Delta G^\circ = -\Delta S^\circ T + \Delta H^\circ$$

Plotting values of ΔG° against T will therefore produce a straight line with gradient equal to $-\Delta S^\circ$.

The graph shows how ΔG° varies with temperature for a particular chemical reaction.

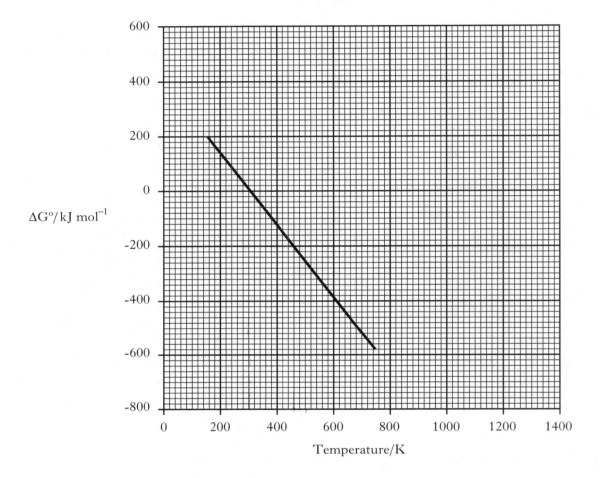

Use the graph to

(a) deduce the temperature at which the reaction just becomes feasible under standard conditions   1

(b) estimate the value of ΔH°, in kJ mol^{-1}, for the reaction   1

(c) calculate the value of ΔS°, in J K^{-1} mol^{-1}.   2

(4)

Marks

7. Consider the three reactions and their rate equations

   Reaction (1) $2N_2O_5 \longrightarrow 4NO_2 + O_2$ Rate = $k[N_2O_5]$

   Reaction (2) $2NO + Cl_2 \longrightarrow 2NOCl$ Rate = $k[NO]^2[Cl_2]$

   Reaction (3) $2NH_3 \longrightarrow N_2 + 3H_2$ Rate = $k[NH_3]^0$

   (a) What is the overall order of Reaction (2)?   1

   (b) The graph below was plotted using experimental results from one of the reactions.

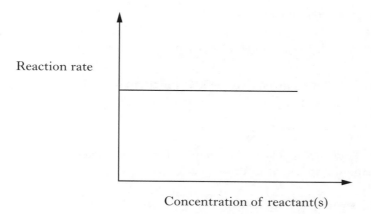

   Explain which of the reactions would give this graph.   1

   (c) For Reaction (2), when the concentrations of NO and Cl_2 are both 0.250 mol l^{-1}, the initial reaction rate is $1.43 \times 10^{-6} \text{ mol l}^{-1} \text{ s}^{-1}$.

   Use this information to calculate the rate constant, k, including the appropriate units.   2

   (4)

8. The reaction between hydrogen peroxide and potassium bromide is used to generate bromine to disinfect water supplies.

   The ion-electron equations involved in this reaction are

   $$Br_2(\ell) + 2e^- \longrightarrow 2Br^-(aq) \qquad E° = 1.07 \text{ V}$$

   $$H_2O_2(aq) + 2H^+(aq) + 2e^- \longrightarrow 2H_2O(\ell) \qquad E° = 1.77 \text{ V}$$

   (a) Write the redox equation for the reaction.   1

   (b) Calculate the standard free energy change, in $kJ \text{ mol}^{-1}$, for this reaction.   3

   (4)

[Turn over

Marks

9. Buffer solutions are important in human biochemistry.

    (a) What is meant by a "buffer solution"?   1

    (b) Suggest the name of a salt which could be mixed with propanoic acid to prepare an acidic buffer solution.   1

    (c) The pH of an alkaline buffer solution can be found using the formula

$$pH = pK_w - pK_b + \log \frac{[base]}{[salt]}$$

    where K_w is the ionic product of water

    and K_b is the dissociation constant of the base.

    $1 \cdot 05 \, g$ of ammonium nitrate, NH_4NO_3, is dissolved in $100 \, cm^3$ of a $0 \cdot 15 \, mol \, l^{-1}$ ammonia solution at $25 \, °C$.

    Calculate the pH of this buffer solution given that the pK_b for ammonia is $4 \cdot 76$.   3

    (5)

10. Chemists are developing compounds which block the ability of certain bacteria to bind to the surface of cells. This will help stop the spread of infection.

    (a) What name is given to the structural fragment of this type of compound which binds to a receptor?   1

    (b) The diagram shows the structure of four of these compounds.

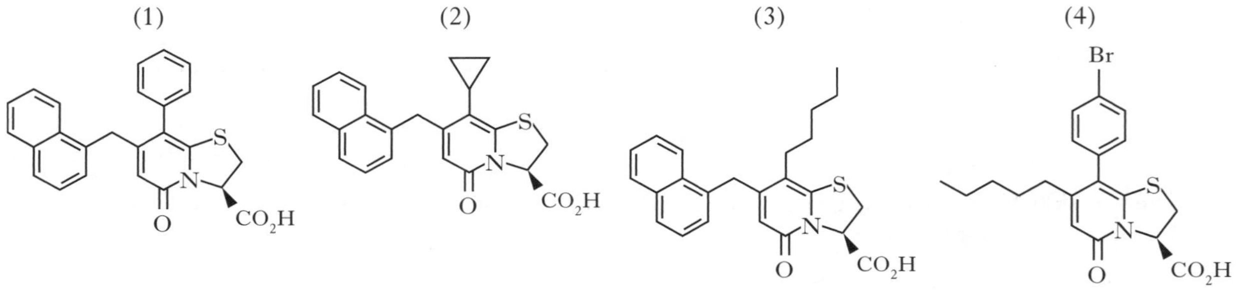

    (1)   (2)   (3)   (4)

    Draw the structural fragment which is common to these compounds which allows them to bind to the relevant receptor.   1

    (2)

Marks

11. Meldrum's acid is a chemical named after the Scotsman, Andrew N. Meldrum who was the first to produce it.

    Microanalysis showed that Meldrum's acid has a composition, by mass, of 50% C, 5·6% H, 44·4% O.

    (a) Use the percentage composition to calculate the empirical formula of Meldrum's acid.

      (Working must be shown)   1

    (b) Meldrum initially thought the structure was

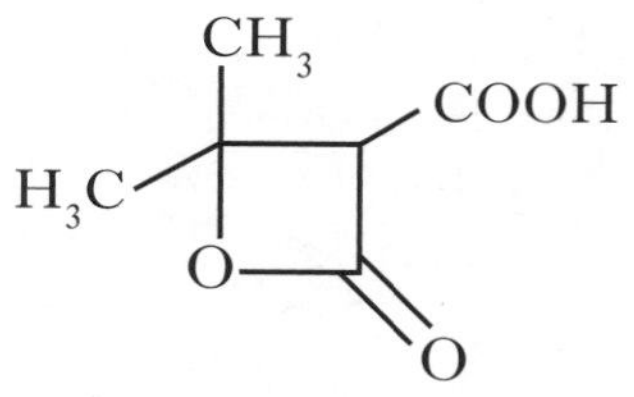

      Compound A

      The structure was later shown to be the isomer of **A** shown below.

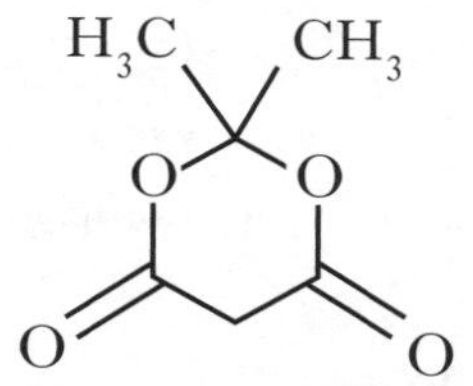

      Compound B

      (i) What is the molecular formula of **A** and **B**?   1

      (ii) The infra-red spectrum of isomer **A** would show a strong absorbance not shown by isomer **B**.

        Identify the wave number range, in cm^{-1}, where this absorbance occurs.   1

                                                                                                      (3)

                                                                                            [Turn over

Marks

12. Cinnamaldehyde is an aromatic compound found in cinnamon. It can also be prepared by the reaction of benzaldehyde and ethanal.

$$C_6H_5CHO + CH_3CHO \rightarrow C_6H_5CHCHCHO$$

   (a) What type of reaction is this?   1

   (b) Draw a full structural formula for cinnamaldehyde.   1

   (c) All three of the carbonyl compounds shown above react with 2,4-dinitrophenylhydrazine, (Brady's reagent), forming solid derivatives.

   The structure of 2,4-dinitrophenylhydrazine is

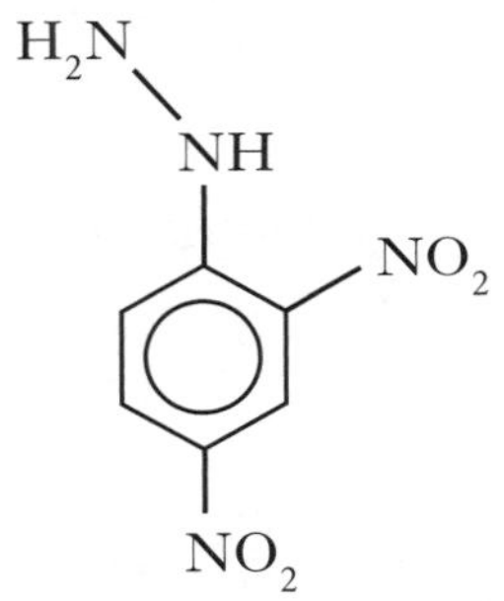

   (i) Draw a structural formula of the compound formed when ethanal reacts with 2,4-dinitrophenylhydrazine.   1

   (ii) The compound formed is impure.

   How would this compound be purified?   1

   (iii) How would the purified compound be used to show that the original carbonyl compound was ethanal?   1

   (iv) 2,4-Dinitrophenylhydrazone derivatives have distinctive colours.

   What colour is the 2,4-dinitrophenylhydrazone derivative of propanone?   1

                                                                                           (6)

13. When sodium hydroxide solution was added to 2-bromomethylpropane an S_N1 reaction took place producing methylpropan-2-ol and hydrobromic acid.

   (a)   (i) What is meant by an S_N1 reaction?   2

         (ii) Draw the structure of the carbocation intermediate formed in this reaction.   1

   (b) Chloromethane reacts with sodium ethoxide in an S_N2 reaction.

       (i) How is sodium ethoxide prepared in the laboratory?   1

       (ii) Name the organic product of this S_N2 reaction.   1

                                                                                           (5)

Marks

14. The structure of lactic acid is

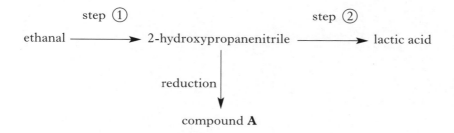

(a) What is the systematic name of lactic acid? 1

(b) Lactic acid contains an asymmetric carbon atom.

Identify, and **explain**, which one of the numbered carbon atoms is asymmetric. 1

(c) Lactic acid can be produced from ethanal by the reaction sequence below.

step ① step ②
ethanal ——————→ 2-hydroxypropanenitrile ——————→ lactic acid

reduction |
↓

compound **A**

(i) Which reagent could be used in step ① ? 1

(ii) What type of reaction takes place in step ② ? 1

(iii) Draw a structure for compound **A**. 1

(5)

[END OF QUESTION PAPER]

[BLANK PAGE]

ADVANCED HIGHER

2012

HODDER
GIBSON
LEARN MORE

[BLANK PAGE]

X012/13/02

NATIONAL
QUALIFICATIONS
2012

MONDAY, 14 MAY
1.00 PM – 3.30 PM

CHEMISTRY
ADVANCED HIGHER

Reference may be made to the Chemistry Higher and Advanced Higher Data Booklet.

SECTION A – 40 marks

Instructions for completion of **SECTION A** are given on page two.

For this section of the examination you must use an **HB pencil.**

SECTION B – 60 marks

All questions should be attempted.

Answers must be written clearly and legibly in ink.

SECTION A

Read carefully

1   Check that the answer sheet provided is for **Chemistry Advanced Higher (Section A)**.

2   For this section of the examination you must use an **HB pencil** and, where necessary, an eraser.

3   Check that the answer sheet you have been given has **your name**, **date of birth**, **SCN** (Scottish Candidate Number) and **Centre Name** printed on it.

Do not change any of these details.

4   If any of this information is wrong, tell the Invigilator immediately.

5   If this information is correct, **print** your name and seat number in the boxes provided.

6   The answer to each question is **either** A, B, C or D. Decide what your answer is, then, using your pencil, put a horizontal line in the space provided (see sample question below).

7   There is **only one correct** answer to each question.

8   Any rough working should be done on the question paper or the rough working sheet, **not** on your answer sheet.

9   At the end of the exam, put the **answer sheet for Section A inside the front cover of your answer book**.

Sample Question

To show that the ink in a ball-pen consists of a mixture of dyes, the method of separation would be

A   chromatography

B   fractional distillation

C   fractional crystallisation

D   filtration.

The correct answer is **A**—chromatography. The answer **A** has been clearly marked in **pencil** with a horizontal line (see below).

Changing an answer

If you decide to change your answer, carefully erase your first answer and using your pencil, fill in the answer you want. The answer below has been changed to **D**.

A   B   C   D

1. Which of the following is **not** a form of electromagnetic radiation?

   A α radiation

   B γ radiation

   C   UV radiation

   D   X-rays

2. An ion, X^{3+}, contains 55 electrons.

   In which block of the Periodic Table would element **X** be found?

   A   s

   B   p

   C   d

   D   f

3. Which of the following statements is **true** about a $Co^{2+}(g)$ ion?

   A   It has 5 unpaired electrons.

   B   It has 8 electrons in s orbitals.

   C   It has 13 electrons in the third shell.

   D   Its electrons with the highest energy are in 3d orbitals.

4. In absorption spectroscopy, as the concentration of an ionic solution decreases, the radiation transmitted

   A   increases in intensity

   B   decreases in intensity

   C   increases in wavelength

   D   decreases in wavelength.

5. Neon gas discharge lamps produce a red glow because electrons in neon atoms are

   A   absorbing radiation from the blue end of the visible spectrum

   B   emitting radiation from the red end of the visible spectrum

   C   emitting radiation from the blue end of the visible spectrum

   D   absorbing radiation from the red end of the visible spectrum.

6. Which of the following molecules has three atoms in a straight line?

   A H_2O

   B SF_6

   C CH_4

   D C_2H_3Br

7. Which of the following ligands is bidentate?

   A CN^-

   B NH_3

   C H_2O

   D $H_2NCH_2CH_2NH_2$

8. $PCl_5 \rightleftharpoons PCl_3 + Cl_2$

   Adding PCl_3 to the above system will

   A   increase the value of the equilibrium constant

   B   decrease the value of the equilibrium constant

   C   increase the concentration of PCl_5 and decrease the concentration of Cl_2

   D   decrease the concentration of PCl_5 and increase the concentration of Cl_2.

9. $AgCl(s) \rightarrow Ag^+(aq) + Cl^-(aq)$

   The solubility product (K_s) for silver chloride is given by the expression

   $$K_s = [Ag^+(aq)] [Cl^-(aq)]$$

   The formula mass of AgCl is 143·4.

   $K_s = 1·80 \times 10^{-10}$ at 25 °C.

   The solubility of silver chloride, in $mol\,l^{-1}$, at 25 °C is

   A $1·80 \times 10^{-10}$

   B $3·60 \times 10^{-10}$

   C $1·34 \times 10^{-5}$

   D $2·68 \times 10^{-5}$.

[Turn over

10. At a particular temperature, $8\cdot0$ mole of NO_2 was placed in a 1 litre container and the NO_2 dissociated by the following reaction:

$$2NO_2(g) \rightleftharpoons 2NO(g) + O_2(g)$$

At equilibrium the concentration of $NO(g)$ is $2\cdot0$ mol l^{-1}.

The equilibrium constant will have a value of

A $0\cdot11$

B $0\cdot22$

C $0\cdot33$

D $9\cdot00$.

11. A buffer solution can **not** be made from

A CH_3CH_2COOH and CH_3CH_2COONa

B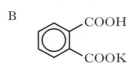

C HNO_3 and $NaNO_3$

D NH_3 and NH_4Cl.

12. $5\cdot0$ cm^3 of a solution of hydrochloric acid was diluted to exactly 250 cm^3 with water. The pH of this diluted solution was $2\cdot00$.

The concentration of the original undiluted solution, in mol l^{-1}, was

A $2\cdot0 \times 10^{-2}$

B $4\cdot0 \times 10^{-2}$

C $4\cdot0 \times 10^{-1}$

D $5\cdot0 \times 10^{-1}$.

13. The graph below shows the pH changes when $0\cdot1$ mol l^{-1} ammonia solution is added to 50 cm^3 of $0\cdot1$ mol l^{-1} hydrochloric acid solution.

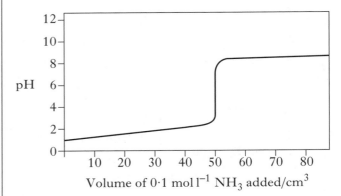

Volume of $0\cdot1$ mol l^{-1} NH_3 added/cm^3

Which line in the table shows an indicator which is **not** suitable for use in determining the equivalence point for the above reaction?

	Indicator	pH range of indicator
A	methyl orange	$3\cdot1 - 4\cdot4$
B	bromophenol red	$5\cdot2 - 6\cdot8$
C	bromothymol blue	$6\cdot0 - 7\cdot6$
D	phenolphthalein	$8\cdot3 - 10\cdot0$

14. $C(s) + O_2(g) \rightarrow CO_2(g)$ $\Delta H^\circ = -396$ kJ mol^{-1}

$Pb(s) + \frac{1}{2}O_2(g) \rightarrow PbO(s)$ $\Delta H^\circ = -210$ kJ mol^{-1}

$PbO(s) + CO(g) \rightarrow Pb(s) + CO_2(g)$ $\Delta H^\circ = -74$ kJ mol^{-1}

What is the value of ΔH°, in kJ mol^{-1}, for the following reaction?

$C(s) + \frac{1}{2}O_2(g) \rightarrow CO(g)$

A -260

B -112

C $+112$

D $+260$

15. $50 \, cm^3$ of $1 \, mol \, l^{-1}$ sodium hydroxide is placed in a beaker.

Which of the following graphs shows how the temperature of the solution in the beaker would change as $100 \, cm^3$ of $1 \, mol \, l^{-1}$ hydrochloric acid is gradually added?

A
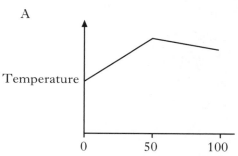

B
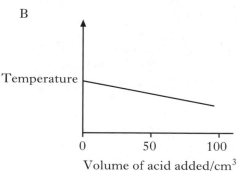

C
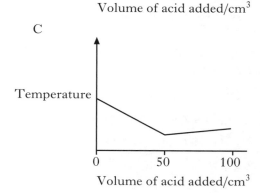

D

16. Which of the following enthalpy changes can **not** be measured directly by experiment?

A Enthalpy of formation of methane

B Enthalpy of combustion of hydrogen

C Enthalpy of formation of carbon dioxide

D Enthalpy of combustion of carbon monoxide

17.

Bond	Bond enthalpy/kJ mol^{-1}
H—H	432
Cl—Cl	243
H—Cl	428

Using the above data, the standard enthalpy of formation of HCl(g), in kJ mol^{-1}, is

A $-90{\cdot}5$

B $-123{\cdot}5$

C -181

D -247.

18. Which of the following equations represents a step that is **not** involved in the Born Haber cycle for the formation of rubidium iodide?

A $I_2(s) \rightarrow I_2(g)$

B $I_2(g) \rightarrow 2I(g)$

C $I(g) \rightarrow I^+(g) + e^-$

D $I(g) + e^- \rightarrow I^-(g)$

19. $Cr^+(g) \rightarrow Cr^{3+}(g) + 2e^-$

The energy required for this change per mole of chromium(III) ions is

A $2259 \, kJ$

B $3000 \, kJ$

C $4600 \, kJ$

D $5259 \, kJ$.

[Turn over

20. For any liquid, $\Delta S_{vapourisation} = \dfrac{\Delta H_{vapourisation}}{T_b}$

where T_b = boiling point of that liquid.

For many liquids,

$\Delta S_{vapourisation} = 88\, J\, K^{-1}\, mol^{-1}$.

Assuming that this value is true for water and that its $\Delta H_{vapourisation} = 40\cdot 6\, kJ\, mol^{-1}$, then the boiling point of water is calculated as

A $0\cdot46\, K$

B $2\cdot17\, K$

C $373\, K$

D $461\, K$.

21. Which line in the table is correct for the enthalpy change and entropy change when steam condenses?

	ΔH	ΔS
A	+ve	+ve
B	+ve	−ve
C	−ve	−ve
D	−ve	+ve

22.

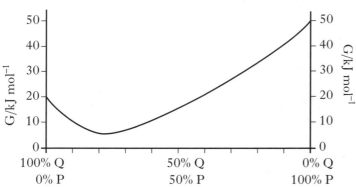

Assuming that liquids P and Q are in their standard states when 100% of either is present, what is the value of ΔG°, in $kJ\, mol^{-1}$, for the reaction represented by the stoichiometric equation,

$$Q(\ell) \rightarrow P(\ell)?$$

A   −15

B   −30

C   +30

D   +45

23. 2-Bromobutane reacts with potassium hydroxide in ethanol to produce two unsaturated products.

The type of reaction involved is

A   addition

B   elimination

C   oxidation

D   substitution.

24. The reaction between chlorine and ethane to give chloroethane is an example of a chain reaction.

Which of the following is a propagation step in this reaction?

A $Cl_2 \rightarrow Cl\bullet + Cl\bullet$

B $C_2H_5\bullet + Cl\bullet \rightarrow C_2H_5Cl$

C $C_2H_5\bullet + C_2H_5\bullet \rightarrow C_4H_{10}$

D $C_2H_5\bullet + Cl_2 \rightarrow C_2H_5Cl + Cl\bullet$

25. Which of the following molecules is likely to produce the most stable carbocation intermediate in a substitution reaction?

A CH_3CH_2I

B $(CH_3)_3CCl$

C CH_3CH_2Cl

D $CH_3CHICH_2CH_3$

26. Which of the following compounds will have the highest boiling point?

A $H-\overset{\overset{\displaystyle H}{|}}{\underset{\underset{\displaystyle H}{|}}{C}}-\overset{\overset{\displaystyle H}{|}}{\underset{\underset{\displaystyle H}{|}}{C}}-\overset{\overset{\displaystyle H}{|}}{\underset{\underset{\displaystyle H}{|}}{C}}-C\overset{\displaystyle O}{\underset{\displaystyle OH}{}}$

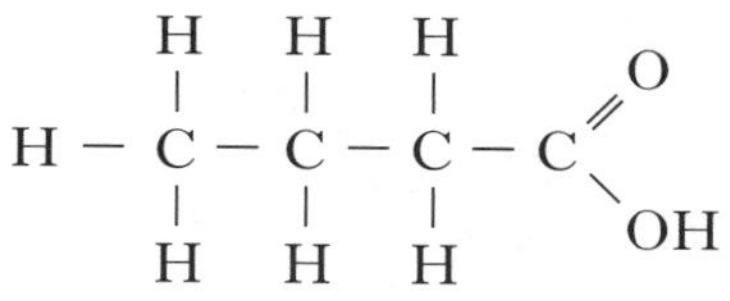

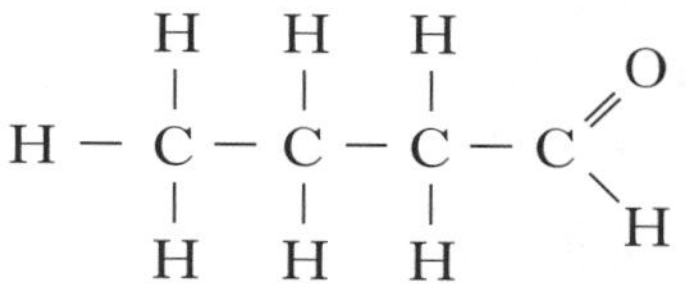

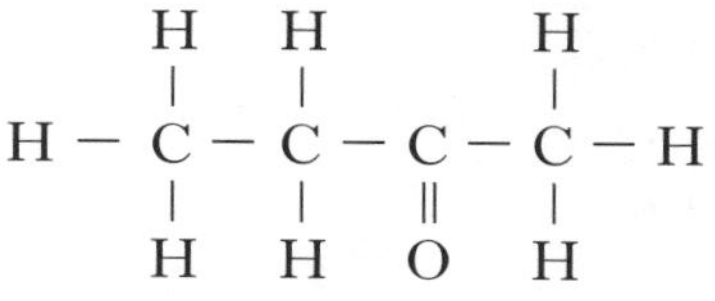

B $H-\overset{\overset{\displaystyle H}{|}}{\underset{\underset{\displaystyle H}{|}}{C}}-\overset{\overset{\displaystyle H}{|}}{\underset{\underset{\displaystyle H}{|}}{C}}-\overset{\overset{\displaystyle H}{|}}{\underset{\underset{\displaystyle H}{|}}{C}}-C\overset{\displaystyle O}{\underset{\displaystyle H}{}}$

C $H-\overset{\overset{\displaystyle H}{|}}{\underset{\underset{\displaystyle H}{|}}{C}}-\overset{\overset{\displaystyle H}{|}}{\underset{\underset{\displaystyle H}{|}}{C}}-\overset{}{\underset{\underset{\displaystyle O}{\|}}{C}}-\overset{\overset{\displaystyle H}{|}}{\underset{\underset{\displaystyle H}{|}}{C}}-H$

D $H-\overset{\overset{\displaystyle H}{|}}{\underset{\underset{\displaystyle H}{|}}{C}}-\overset{\overset{\displaystyle H}{|}}{\underset{\underset{\displaystyle H}{|}}{C}}-\overset{\overset{\displaystyle H}{|}}{\underset{\underset{\displaystyle H}{|}}{C}}-\overset{\overset{\displaystyle H}{|}}{\underset{\underset{\displaystyle H}{|}}{C}}-OH$

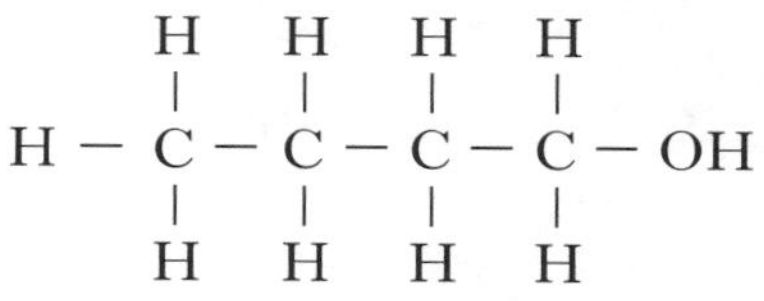

27. Which of the following is an **essential** property of a solvent to be used for recrystallisation purposes?

   A   Insoluble in water

   B   A low boiling point

   C   Ability to dissolve more solute when hot than when cold

   D   Ability to dissolve more solute when cold than when hot

28. Which of the following is correct for the reaction of propene with hydrogen bromide?

   A   1-Bromopropane is the only product.

   B   1-Bromopropane is the major product.

   C   2-Bromopropane is the only product.

   D   2-Bromopropane is the major product.

29. Hybrid orbitals can be formed by the mixing of s and p orbitals.

   Which of the following hybrid orbitals are most likely to be involved in the bonding in ethyne?

   A   sp

   B sp^2

   C sp^3

   D s^2p

30. Carbon dioxide has the following structure.

   $$O = C = O$$

   Which line in the table shows the correct numbers of σ and π bonds in a molecule of carbon dioxide?

	Number of σ bonds	Number of π bonds
A	0	2
B	2	2
C	4	0
D	0	4

31. P $\bigcirc$—Cl

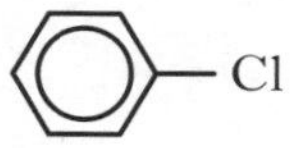

   Q $CH_2=CHCl$

   R $CH_2=CHCH_2Cl$

   Which of the above molecules is/are planar?

   A   **P** only

   B   **P** and **Q** only

   C   **Q** and **R** only

   D   **P**, **Q** and **R**

[Turn over

32. Which of the following can be distinguished by making 2,4-dinitrophenylhydrazone derivatives?

   A   Ethanal and propanal

   B   Propan-1-ol and propan-2-ol

   C   Ethanoic acid and benzoic acid

   D   Methoxyethane and ethoxyethane

33. Which of the following could be the molecular formula for a ketone?

   A C_3H_8O

   B C_3H_6O

   C C_2H_4O

   D CH_2O

34. Which of the following compounds would dissolve in water to give an alkaline solution?

   A CH_3CH_2CN

   B CH_3CH_2CHO

   C $CH_3CH_2CH_2OH$

   D $CH_3CH_2CH_2NH_2$

35.

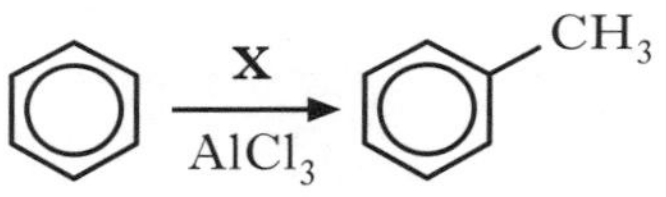

   Which of the following compounds could be **X**?

   A CH_4

   B CH_3Cl

   C CH_2Cl_2

   D CH_3OH

36. Which of the following has a geometric isomer?

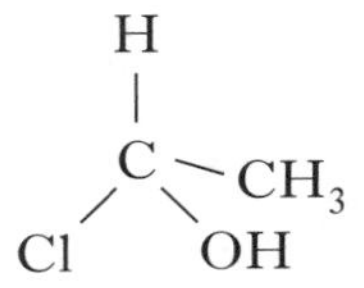

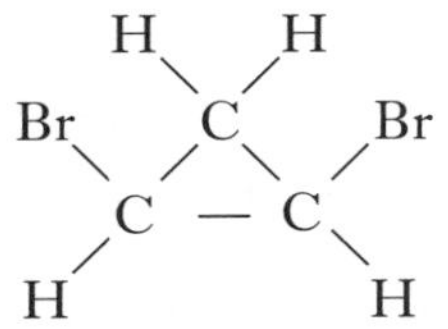

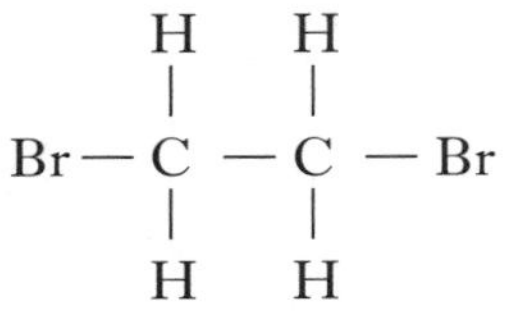

37. Combustion analysis of hydrocarbon **X** showed that it contained 82·7% carbon and 17·3% hydrogen.

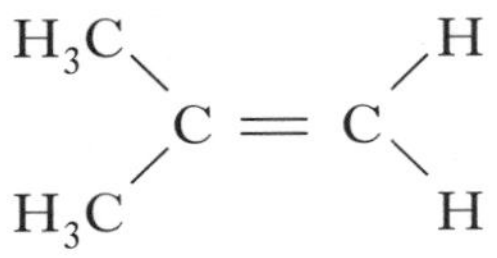

   The molecular formula for **X** could be

   A CH_3

   B C_2H_6

   C C_2H_5

   D C_4H_{10}.

38. The number of waves per centimetre is known as the

   A   wavenumber

   B   wavelength

   C   frequency

   D   intensity.

39. Which of the following analytical techniques depends on the vibrations within molecules?

    A   Colorimetry

    B   Mass spectroscopy

    C   Proton nmr spectroscopy

    D   Infra-red absorption spectroscopy

40.

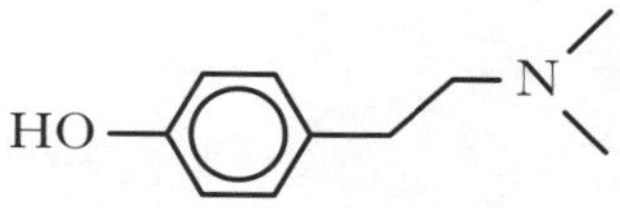

The active structural fragment of several pain-killing molecules is shown.

What term best describes this structural fragment?

    A   Agonist

    B   Receptor

    C   Antagonist

    D   Pharmacophore

[END OF SECTION A]

Candidates are reminded that the answer sheet for Section A MUST be placed INSIDE the front cover of your answer book.

[Turn over for SECTION B on *Page ten*

SECTION B

Marks

60 marks are available in this section of the paper.

All answers must be written clearly and legibly in ink.

1. Semiconductors are used in a wide variety of applications.

   (a) In Blu-ray DVD players, light of wavelength 405 nm is produced from a gallium(III) nitride laser.

      (i) Calculate the energy, in kJ mol^{-1}, corresponding to this wavelength.   2

      (ii) Write the electronic configuration of gallium(III) in terms of s, p and d orbitals.   1

   (b) The electrical conductivity of the semiconductor gallium arsenide increases on exposure to light.

   What name is given to this phenomenon?   1

   (c) Doped silicon is also used as a semiconductor.

   What is the main current carrier in silicon doped with boron?   1

                                                                        (5)

2. The nitrate ion, NO_3^-, can be converted into either nitrous acid, HNO_2 or nitrogen monoxide, NO.

   The oxidation state of nitrogen in NO is +2.

   (a) Calculate the oxidation state of nitrogen in

      (i) NO_3^-

      (ii) HNO_2.   1

   (b) Write a balanced ion-electron equation for the reduction of nitrous acid into the compound $H_2N_2O_2$.   1

   (c) Nitrogen is also present in the cyanide ion, CN^-.

   Name the complex ion $[Cu(CN)_2]^-$.   1

                                                                        (3)

Marks

3. Two common crystal lattice structures adopted by ionic compounds can be described as simple cubic and face-centred cubic.

   (*a*) What determines the type of structure adopted by a particular ionic compound?   1

   (*b*) Sodium chloride has a face-centred cubic structure which has 6:6 coordination.

        Explain what 6:6 coordination means.   1

   (*c*) Caesium chloride has a simple cubic structure which has 8:8 coordination.

        Which potassium halide is most likely to have 8:8 coordination?   1

   (*d*) Many ionic compounds are soluble in water.

      (i) Which two factors determine whether the enthalpy of solution is exothermic or endothermic?   1

      (ii) The enthalpy of solution of sodium chloride is 0 kJ mol^{-1}.

           Suggest what makes the dissolving of sodium chloride in water a feasible process.   1

                                   (5)

4. BH_3 in the gas phase is very reactive. It readily combines with the compound tetrahydrofuran, C_4H_8O, to make a more stable compound.

$$BH_3 + C_4H_8O \rightarrow C_4H_8OBH_3$$

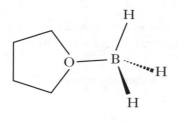

   (*a*) What is the shape of a BH_3 molecule?   1

   (*b*) In the more stable compound a dative covalent bond exists between the boron and oxygen.

        How does this dative covalent bond form?   1

   (*c*) To which class of organic compound does tetrahydrofuran belong?   1

                                   (3)

[Turn over

Marks

5. As part of an investigation a student was analysing the metallic content of a key known to be composed of a copper/nickel alloy.

The key was dissolved in nitric acid and the resulting solution diluted to $1000\,cm^3$ in a standard flask using tap water. Three $25 \cdot 0\,cm^3$ samples of the nitrate solution were pipetted into separate conical flasks and approximately $10\,g$ of solid potassium iodide were added. Iodine was produced as shown in the equation.

$$2Cu^{2+}(aq) + 4I^-(aq) \rightarrow 2CuI(s) + I_2(aq)$$

The liberated iodine was titrated against standardised $0 \cdot 102\,mol\,l^{-1}$ sodium thiosulphate solution. Starch indicator was added near the end point of the titration.

$$I_2(aq) + 2S_2O_3^{2-}(aq) \rightarrow 2I^-(aq) + S_4O_6^{2-}(aq)$$

The results, for the volume of thiosulphate used, are given in the table.

	Titration 1	Titration 2	Titration 3
Final volume/cm^3	16·30	31·50	46·80
Initial volume/cm^3	0·30	16·30	31·50
Volume added/cm^3	16·00	15·20	15·30

(a) From the results calculate the mass of copper in the key.   3

(b) Suggest how the accuracy of the analysis could be improved.   1

(c) The student then tried to analyse the original nitrate solution for nickel using EDTA as in a PPA experiment. The value obtained for the nickel content was much greater than the true value.

Give the main reason why the value obtained was higher than the true value.   1

(5)

Marks

6. A student was trying to determine the partition coefficient of propanedioic acid between the two solvents, hexane and water.

$$\text{propanedioic acid}_{(water)} \rightleftharpoons \text{propanedioic acid}_{(hexane)}$$

The following series of steps were carried out.

Step A. 25 cm^3 water and 25 cm^3 hexane were pipetted into apparatus X.

Step B. A measured mass of propanedioic acid was added to the solvents in apparatus X.

Step C. The mixture was shaken for approximately 2 minutes and allowed to settle.

These steps were repeated with different masses of propanedioic acid.

(a) Name apparatus X. 　1

(b) A series of titrations were carried out which enabled the student to work out the equilibrium concentrations of propanedioic acid in the two solvents. The values obtained are given in the table below.

Mass of propanedioic acid used/g	Concentration of propanedioic acid in water/mol l^{-1}	Concentration of propanedioic acid in hexane/mol l^{-1}
0·31	0·24	0·031
0·44	0·30	0·038
0·61	0·37	0·048

Use these results to calculate a value for the partition coefficient. 　1

(c) The student repeated the experiment several weeks later using the same chemicals. The values obtained are given in the table below.

Mass of propanedioic acid used/g	Concentration of propanedioic acid in water/mol l^{-1}	Concentration of propanedioic acid in hexane/mol l^{-1}
0·93	0·57	0·083

Give the reason why this experiment produces a different value for the partition coefficient compared to the value calculated earlier. 　1

(d) Why would no partition take place if ethanol had been used instead of hexane? 　1

　(4)

[Turn over

Marks

7. Balsamic vinegar is a dark brown liquid containing ethanoic acid. The pH of a sample of balsamic vinegar was 2·5.

    (a) Calculate the concentration of ethanoic acid in the sample of balsamic vinegar.   2

    (b) A student chose to use a pH meter rather than use an indicator for the titration of balsamic vinegar with sodium hydroxide.

    Apart from being more accurate, suggest why the student chose to use a pH meter rather than an indicator for this particular titration.   1

    (c) Write the formula for the conjugate base of ethanoic acid.   1

    (4)

8. Part of an Ellingham diagram is shown below.

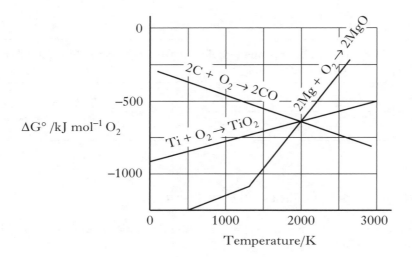

    (a) Using the Ellingham diagram give the temperature **range** over which magnesium will reduce titanium dioxide to titanium.   1

    (b) Suggest why the line labelled $2C + O_2 \rightarrow 2CO$ slopes downward.   1

    (c) Suggest why the gradient of the line labelled $2Mg + O_2 \rightarrow 2MgO$ changes at approximately 1360 K.   1

    (3)

9. Silver oxide cells are used in hearing aids. Zinc is the negative electrode and silver(I) oxide is the positive electrode. The overall cell reaction is represented by the equation

    $$Zn(s) + Ag_2O(s) \rightarrow ZnO(s) + 2Ag(s)$$

    The free energy change for the cell is −279·8 kJ per mole of zinc.

    Calculate the voltage produced by the cell.   **(3)**

Marks

10. The graphs show how the concentrations of reactants A and B change with time for the reaction

$$A + B \rightarrow C$$

Using a large excess of B

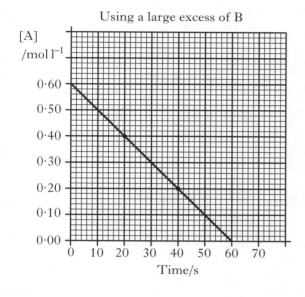

Using a large excess of A

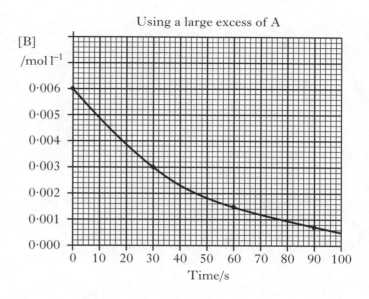

(a) What is the order of reaction with respect to A?   **1**

(b) What is the order of reaction with respect to B?   **1**

(c) What are the units of the rate constant in this reaction?   **1**

(3)

11. Both lithium aluminium hydride, $LiAlH_4$, and phosphorus pentachloride, PCl_5, react vigorously with water producing different gases.

(a) Name the gas produced when water reacts with

    (i) lithium aluminium hydride   **1**

    (ii) phosphorus pentachloride.   **1**

(b) Phosphorus pentachloride will also react with any compound containing a hydroxyl group. A chlorine atom replaces the hydroxyl group. For example,

$$C_6H_5COOH \xrightarrow{\ PCl_5\ } C_6H_5COCl \quad \text{or} \quad CH_3COOH \xrightarrow{\ PCl_5\ } CH_3COCl$$

    (i) What type of organic compound is produced in these reactions?   **1**

    (ii) Draw a structural formula for the ester formed when C_6H_5COCl reacts with propan-2-ol.   **1**

    (iii) What is the advantage of using C_6H_5COCl instead of benzoic acid in this esterification reaction?   **1**

(5)

Marks

12. Skeletal structural formulae are used to show structures of molecules more simply than full structural formulae.

For example, pent-1-ene can be represented as

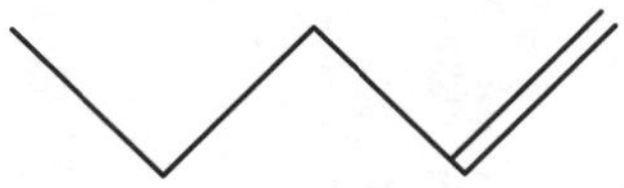

and butan-2-ol as

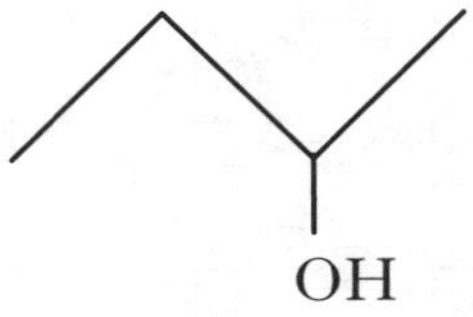

Lipoic acid has recently been used as a food supplement. The skeletal structural formula of lipoic acid is shown below.

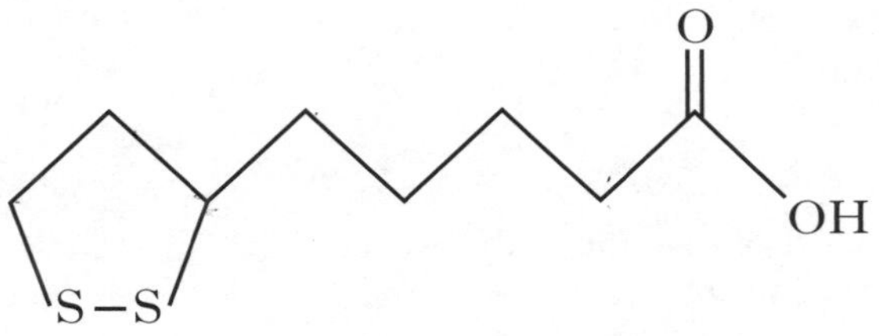

(a) Write the molecular formula of lipoic acid.   **1**

(b) (i) Lipoic acid is optically active. Copy the skeletal structural formula of lipoic acid and circle the carbon atom responsible for the optical activity of lipoic acid.   **1**

    (ii) Why does this carbon atom make lipoic acid optically active?   **1**

                                                                                              (3)

Marks

13. In a PPA, benzoic acid is prepared from ethyl benzoate by refluxing with sodium hydroxide solution.

gfm = 150 g   gfm = 122 g

(a) Why is the mixture refluxed rather than heated in an open beaker?   1

(b) Name the type of reaction that is involved between ethyl benzoate and sodium hydroxide solution.   1

(c) What does the procedure suggest should be added to the flask along with ethyl benzoate and sodium hydroxide solution?   1

(d) What change in appearance of the contents of the flask indicates that the reaction is complete?   1

(e) A yield of 73·2% of benzoic acid was obtained from 5·64 g of ethyl benzoate.

Calculate the mass of benzoic acid produced.   2

(6)

14. (a) Benzene reacts with a "nitrating mixture" to produce nitrobenzene.

(i) Name the type of chemical reaction that takes place in the nitration of benzene.   1

(ii) Nitrobenzene is reduced by reaction with a mixture of tin and concentrated hydrochloric acid to form an organic base.

Identify this organic base.   1

(b) Benzene also reacts with sulphur trioxide dissolved in concentrated sulphuric acid to produce benzenesulphonic acid, $C_6H_5SO_3H$.

(i) Draw a structural formula for benzenesulphonic acid.   1

(ii) Draw a Lewis electron dot diagram for sulphur trioxide.   1

(4)

[Turn over for Question 15 on *Page eighteen*

Marks

15. Chloroalkane **A** has molecular formula C_4H_9Cl. When **A** is heated with NaOH(aq), it undergoes an S_N2 reaction to form alcohol **B**.

    Alcohol **B** can be oxidised by acidified potassium dichromate solution and it can also be dehydrated to produce a mixture of two alkenes which are structural isomers.

    (*a*) Draw a structural formula for compound **A**.   1

    (*b*) Draw the structure of the transition state involved in this S_N2 reaction.   1

    (*c*) The simplified proton nmr spectrum of one of the alkenes is shown.

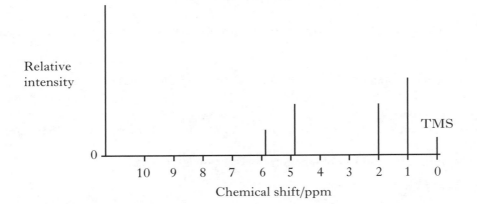

    Sketch the proton nmr spectrum of the other alkene.   2

    (4)

[END OF QUESTION PAPER]

ADVANCED HIGHER

2013

[BLANK PAGE]

X012/13/02

NATIONAL
QUALIFICATIONS
2013

FRIDAY, 31 MAY
1.00 PM – 3.30 PM

CHEMISTRY
ADVANCED HIGHER

Reference may be made to the Chemistry Higher and Advanced Higher Data Booklet.

SECTION A – 40 marks

Instructions for completion of **SECTION A** are given on page two.

For this section of the examination you must use an **HB pencil.**

SECTION B – 60 marks

All questions should be attempted.

Answers must be written clearly and legibly in ink.

SECTION A

Read carefully

1   Check that the answer sheet provided is for **Chemistry Advanced Higher (Section A)**.

2   For this section of the examination you must use an **HB pencil** and, where necessary, an eraser.

3   Check that the answer sheet you have been given has **your name**, **date of birth**, **SCN** (Scottish Candidate Number) and **Centre Name** printed on it.

    Do not change any of these details.

4   If any of this information is wrong, tell the Invigilator immediately.

5   If this information is correct, **print** your name and seat number in the boxes provided.

6   The answer to each question is **either** A, B, C or D. Decide what your answer is, then, using your pencil, put a horizontal line in the space provided (see sample question below).

7   There is **only one correct** answer to each question.

8   Any rough working should be done on the question paper or the rough working sheet, **not** on your answer sheet.

9   At the end of the exam, put the **answer sheet for Section A inside the front cover of your answer book**.

Sample Question

To show that the ink in a ball-pen consists of a mixture of dyes, the method of separation would be

      A   chromatography

      B   fractional distillation

      C   fractional crystallisation

      D   filtration.

The correct answer is **A**—chromatography. The answer **A** has been clearly marked in **pencil** with a horizontal line (see below).

Changing an answer

If you decide to change your answer, carefully erase your first answer and using your pencil, fill in the answer you want. The answer below has been changed to **D**.

1. Which equation can be used to represent the second ionisation energy of the diatomic element, X?

   A $X_2(g) \rightarrow X_2^{2+}(g) + 2e^-$

   B $\frac{1}{2}X_2(g) \rightarrow X^{2+}(g) + 2e^-$

   C $X^+(g) \rightarrow X^{2+}(g) + e^-$

   D $X(g) \rightarrow X^{2+}(g) + 2e^-$

2. Which of the following lists electromagnetic radiation bands in order of increasing frequency?

   A   Ultraviolet, visible, infra-red, radio

   B   Radio, infra-red, visible, ultraviolet

   C   Radio, microwave, ultraviolet, visible

   D   Visible, ultraviolet, X-ray, microwave

3. Using information from the Data Booklet which one of the following metal salts will emit radiation of the highest frequency when placed in a Bunsen flame?

   A   Copper(II) sulphate

   B   Potassium chloride

   C   Barium chloride

   D   Lithium sulphate

4. Which of the following indicators transmits only the lower frequencies of the visible spectrum at low pH?

Indicator	Colour in acid	Colour in alkali
A	Violet	Red
B	Green	Blue
C	Yellow	Violet
D	Red	Yellow

5. When electrons occupy degenerate orbitals, they do so in such a way as to maximise the number of parallel spins. This statement is known as

   A   the Pauli exclusion principle

   B   Heisenberg's uncertainty principle

   C   the aufbau principle

   D   Hund's rule.

6. Which of the following represents the configuration of the highest energy electrons in an atom of a Group III element in the ground state?

   A $3s^2 3p^1$

   B $3s^2 3p^3$

   C $4s^2 3d^1$

   D $4s^2 4p^3$

7. Which of the following analytical techniques would be most suitable to determine quantitatively the concentration of sodium ions in a urine sample?

   A   Mass spectrometry

   B   Infra-red spectroscopy

   C   Atomic emission spectroscopy

   D   Proton nuclear magnetic resonance spectroscopy

8. Which of the following represents a valid Lewis electron dot diagram for ozone, O_3?

   A

   B

   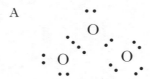

   C

   D

9. Which of the following substances contains a dative covalent bond?

   A NH_3

   B NCl_3

   C NH_4Cl

   D CH_3NH_2

10. Which of the following molecules has the greatest number of non-bonding electron pairs (lone pairs)?

   A
   $$H-\overset{\overset{\displaystyle H}{|}}{C}=O$$

   B
   $$H-\overset{\overset{\displaystyle H}{|}}{\underset{\underset{\displaystyle H}{|}}{C}}-Cl$$

   C
   $$H-\overset{\overset{\displaystyle H}{|}}{\underset{\underset{\displaystyle H}{|}}{C}}-N\overset{\nearrow H}{\searrow_H}$$

   D
   $$H-\overset{\overset{\displaystyle H}{|}}{\underset{\underset{\displaystyle H}{|}}{C}}-O-H$$

11. The following diagram represents a square-planar structure.

   Where ◣──◣ and ◁──◁ represent bonding electron pairs

   and ⊙ represents a non-bonding electron pair (lone pair).

   Which of the following species could have the structure shown above?

   A SF_4

   B NH_4^+

   C XeF_4

   D AlH_4^-

12.

   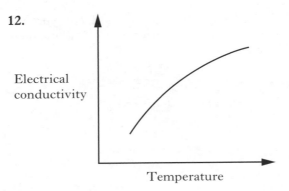

   The graph shows how the electrical conductivity varies with temperature in

   A   a metal

   B   an ionic solid

   C   a semiconductor

   D   a superconductor.

13. Which of the following compounds contains hydride ions?

   A NH_3

   B HCl

   C H_2S

   D CaH_2

14. In which of the following reactions does the oxidation state of copper neither increase nor decrease?

   A $Zn + CuSO_4 \rightarrow ZnSO_4 + Cu$

   B $CuSO_4 + 4NH_3 \rightarrow [Cu(NH_3)_4]SO_4$

   C $FeCl_2 + CuCl_2 \rightarrow FeCl_3 + CuCl$

   D $Cu + 4HNO_3 \rightarrow Cu(NO_3)_2 + 2H_2O + 2NO_2$

15. $100\,cm^3$ of $0\cdot500\,mol\,l^{-1}$ $AgNO_3(aq)$ is reacted with excess $CaCl_2(aq)$.

   What mass of precipitate forms?

   A $7\cdot17\,g$

   B $8\cdot95\,g$

   C $12\cdot6\,g$

   D $14\cdot3\,g$

16. When a salt, formula $Ni(H_2O)_6.K_2(SO_4)_2$, is dissolved in water, the solution contains the ions $Ni(H_2O)_6^{2+}$, K^+ and SO_4^{2-}.

    The total number of moles of ions in one litre of 0.01 mol l^{-1} solution is

    A 0.01

    B 0.03

    C 0.05

    D 0.10.

17. What volume of 0.2 mol l^{-1} potassium sulphate is required to make, by dilution with water, one litre of a solution with a **potassium** ion concentration of 0.1 mol l^{-1}?

    A $100\ cm^3$

    B $250\ cm^3$

    C $400\ cm^3$

    D $500\ cm^3$

18. Phosphoric acid is a weak acid and undergoes partial dissociation according to the equation

    $$H_3PO_4 \rightleftharpoons H_2PO_4^- + H^+$$

    The position of equilibrium would be shifted to the right by the addition of

    A   a catalyst

    B   sulphuric acid

    C   sodium hydroxide

    D   sodium dihydrogenphosphate.

19. Caffeine can be extracted from coffee dissolved in water using the solvent dichloromethane (CH_2Cl_2).

    $$caffeine(aq) \rightleftharpoons caffeine(CH_2Cl_2)$$

    Which of the following, when increased, will change the value of the partition coefficient for this equilibrium?

    A   Temperature

    B   Mass of coffee

    C   Volume of water

    D   Volume of dichloromethane

20. Substance **X** is distributed between equal volumes of two immiscible liquids as shown in the diagram. The number of dots represents the relative distribution of **X** in the two liquids at equilibrium.

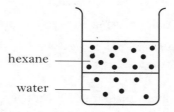

    $$\mathbf{X}(aq) \rightleftharpoons \mathbf{X}(hexane)$$

    The partition coefficient for this system is

    A 0.46

    B 0.50

    C 2.00

    D 2.17.

21. Which of the following decreases when an aqueous solution of ethanoic acid is diluted?

    A   pH

    B $[H^+]$

    C   pKa

    D   The degree of dissociation

22. Iodide ions are oxidised by acidified nitrite ions according to the equation

    $$2NO_2^- + 2I^- + 4H^+ \rightarrow 2NO + I_2 + 2H_2O$$

    Addition of sodium ethanoate to the reaction mixture slows down the formation of iodine.

    The most likely explanation for this effect is that ethanoate ions

    A   remove iodine

    B   reduce the concentration of iodide ions

    C   react with nitrite ions

    D   react with hydrogen ions.

[Turn over

23. Which of the following indicators should be used in the titration of potassium hydroxide solution with ethanoic acid solution?

A   Phenolphthalein, pH range $8 \cdot 0 - 9 \cdot 8$

B   Bromothymol blue, pH range $6 \cdot 0 - 7 \cdot 6$

C   Methyl red, pH range $4 \cdot 2 - 6 \cdot 2$

D   Methyl orange, pH range $3 \cdot 1 - 4 \cdot 4$

24. The following diagram illustrates the catalysed and uncatalysed reaction pathways for a reversible reaction.

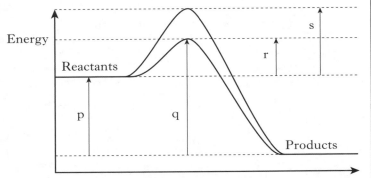

The activation energy for the reverse uncatalysed reaction is given by

A $s - r$

B $p + s$

C $q - p$

D $p + r.$

25. The element X can exist in two forms, as $X \equiv X$, or as X_8 with the following cubic structure.

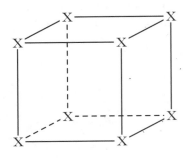

The X—X bond dissociation enthalpy is $163 \, kJ \, mol^{-1}$.
The $X \equiv X$ bond dissociation enthalpy is $944 \, kJ \, mol^{-1}$.

Which of the following is the value of ΔH, in $kJ \, mol^{-1}$, for the reaction

$$X_8(g) \rightarrow 4X_2(g)?$$

A -2472

B -1820

C $+1820$

D $+2472$

26. Which of the following sets of information would enable the bond enthalpy of a C=C double bond to be calculated?

	Enthalpy of formation of	Enthalpy of combustion of	Enthalpy of sublimation of	(Mean) bond enthalpy of
A	ethene	ethene		C—H, H—H
B	benzene	benzene		C—H, H—H
C	ethene		carbon	C—H, H—H
D	benzene		carbon	C—H, H—H

27. In which of the following changes will there be an increase in entropy?

   A $CO_2(g) \rightarrow CO_2(s)$

   B   Combustion of ethanol

   C   Hydrogenation of ethene

   D   Phenylethene $\rightarrow$ poly(phenylethene)

28. One mole of which of the following chlorides would have the greatest entropy at **750 °C**?

   A   Sodium chloride

   B   Calcium chloride

   C   Potassium chloride

   D   Magnesium chloride

29. The conversion of butanoic acid into butan-1-ol is an example of

   A   elimination

   B   substitution

   C   oxidation

   D   reduction.

30.

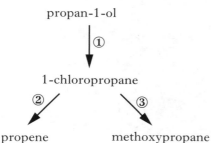

   propan-1-ol
   ①
   1-chloropropane
   ②   ③
   propene   methoxypropane

   Which line in the table is correct for the types of reaction taking place at ①, ② and ③?

	Reaction ①	Reaction ②	Reaction ③
A	substitution	elimination	substitution
B	substitution	reduction	substitution
C	addition	reduction	condensation
D	addition	elimination	substitution

31. Bromine reacts with propene to produce 1,2-dibromopropane.

   A possible intermediate in the reaction is

   A   (structure: propane chain with ⊕ on central carbon and Br on end carbon)

   B   (structure: propane chain with Br on central carbon and ⊕ on end carbon)

   C   (structure: propane chain with Br bridging, ⊖ charge)

   D   (structure: propane chain with Br bridging, ⊕ charge)

32. Which of the following represents an initiation step in a chain reaction?

   A $Cl_2 \rightarrow 2Cl\bullet$

   B $CH_3\bullet + CH_3\bullet \rightarrow C_2H_6$

   C $CH_4 + Cl\bullet \rightarrow CH_3Cl + H\bullet$

   D $CH_3\bullet + Cl_2 \rightarrow CH_3Cl + Cl\bullet$

33. Which of the following compounds would be expected to have the highest boiling point?

   A   Pentanal

   B   Pentan-2-ol

   C   Pentan-2-one

   D   Ethoxypropane

[Turn over

34. Which line in the table shows a general formula which does **not** match the homologous series?

	General formula	Homologous series
A	$C_nH_{2n}O$	alkanals
B	$C_nH_{2n}O_2$	alkanoic acids
C	$C_nH_{2n+2}O$	alkanols
D	$C_nH_{2n}O$	ethers

35. The Williamson synthesis for the preparation of unsymmetrical ethers (ROR′) starting with an alcohol and a halogenoalkane is summarised in the general equations:

Step 1: $ROH + Na \rightarrow RO^-Na^+ + \frac{1}{2}H_2$

Step 2: $RO^-Na^+ + R'X \rightarrow ROR' + Na^+X^-$

Using propan-2-ol and 2-chlorobutane, the unsymmetrical ether formed would be

A $CH_3CH_2CH_2OCH(CH_3)CH_2CH_3$

B $CH_3CH_2CH_2OCH_2CH_2CH_2CH_3$

C $CH_3CH(CH_3)OCH_2CH_2CH_2CH_3$

D $CH_3CH(CH_3)OCH(CH_3)CH_2CH_3$

36. Which of the following is the strongest base?

A CH_3CH_2OH

B   ⟨◯⟩— OH

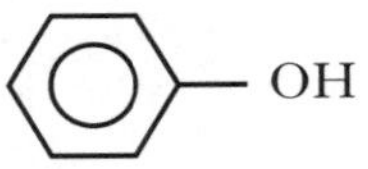

C $CH_3CH_2NH_2$

D   ⟨◯⟩— NH_2

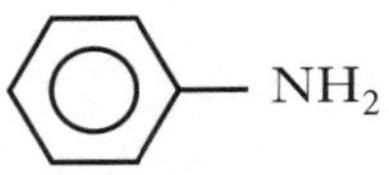

37. Phenylamine reacts with hydrochloric acid.

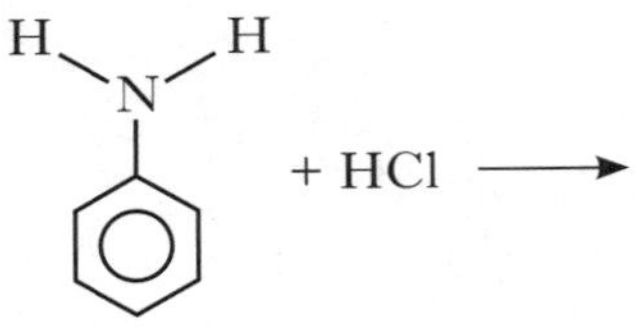

The products are

A

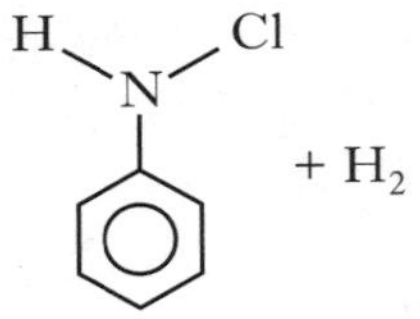

B

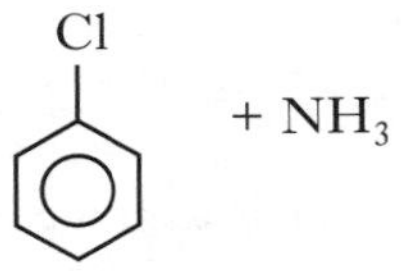

C

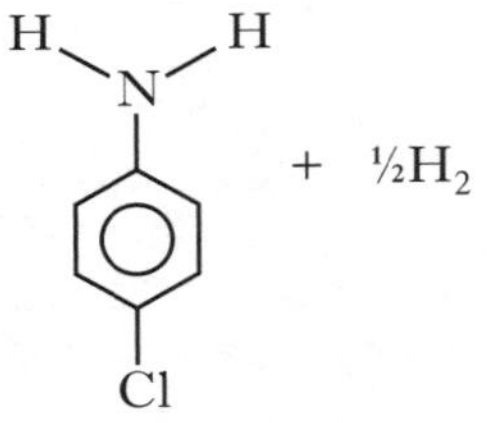

D

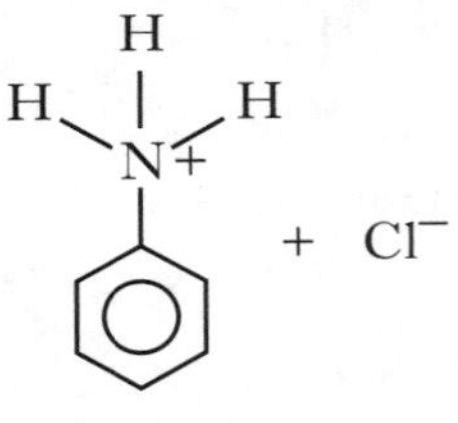

38.

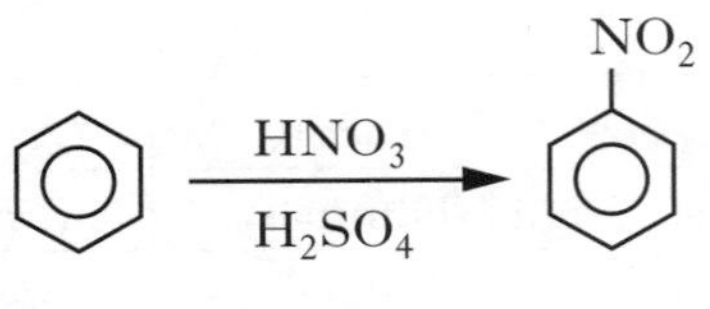

Which species initially attacks the benzene molecule in the above reaction?

A NO_3^-

B NO_2^+

C HSO_4^-

D NO_2

39.

The above reaction is an example of

A   addition

B   oxidation

C   elimination

D   substitution.

40. Most medicines work by binding to receptors.

Receptors are usually

A   nucleophiles

B   electrophiles

C   free radicals

D   protein molecules.

[*END OF SECTION A*]

Candidates are reminded that the answer sheet for Section A MUST be placed INSIDE the front cover of your answer book.

[Turn over for SECTION B on *Page ten*

SECTION B   *Marks*

60 marks are available in this section of the paper.

All answers must be written clearly and legibly in ink.

1. (*a*)   Name a dopant which could be added to germanium to make a p-type semiconductor.   **1**

    (*b*)   What is the charge carrier in a p-type semiconductor?   **1**

                                                                                          (2)

2. Burning magnesium continues to burn when placed in a gas jar of carbon dioxide according to the equation

    $$2Mg(s) + CO_2(g) \rightarrow 2MgO(s) + C(s)$$

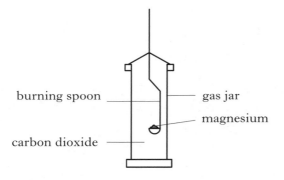

Substance	$S°/JK^{-1}\,mol^{-1}$
Mg(s)	33·0
CO_2(g)	214
MgO(s)	27·0
C(s)	5·70

    (*a*)   Using the values from the table above, calculate $\Delta S°$ for the reaction.   **1**

    (*b*)   Using the information below and your answer to (*a*), calculate $\Delta G°$ for the burning of magnesium in carbon dioxide.

    $$Mg(s) + \tfrac{1}{2}O_2(g) \rightarrow MgO(s) \qquad \Delta H° = -493 \text{ kJ mol}^{-1}$$

    $$C(s) + O_2(g) \rightarrow CO_2(g) \qquad \Delta H° = -394 \text{ kJ mol}^{-1}$$ **3**

                                                                                          (4)

Marks

3. The Born-Haber cycle diagram shows the theoretical process involved in the formation of rubidium chloride from the elements rubidium and chlorine.

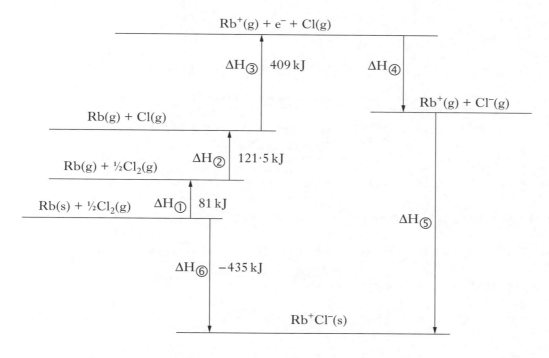

(a) Write the equation which represents the standard enthalpy of formation of rubidium chloride.   **1**

(b) Use the Data Booklet to find the value for enthalpy change $\Delta H_④$.   **1**

(c) What name is given to the enthalpy change represented by $\Delta H_⑤$?   **1**

(d) Calculate the value for enthalpy change $\Delta H_⑤$.   **1**

          (4)

4. In a PPA the manganese content of a steel paper clip is determined by converting the manganese into purple permanganate ions, the concentration of which is measured using colorimetry.

   At the start of the activity, a calibration graph has to be drawn.

   (a) What data must be collected to allow the calibration graph to be drawn?   **1**

   (b) Which colour of filter or wavelength of light should be used in this procedure?   **1**

   (c) A weighed sample of the paper clip is dissolved in $2 \, mol \, l^{-1}$ nitric acid in a beaker covered with a watch glass which is placed in a fume cupboard because a toxic gas is produced.

   Name this toxic gas.   **1**

   (d) Colorimetry is not used to determine potassium content because potassium ions are not coloured. The concentration of potassium ions in a compound can be determined using atomic absorption spectroscopy at a wavelength of 405 nm.

   Calculate the energy, in $kJ \, mol^{-1}$, of this radiation.   **2**

          (5)

Marks

5.

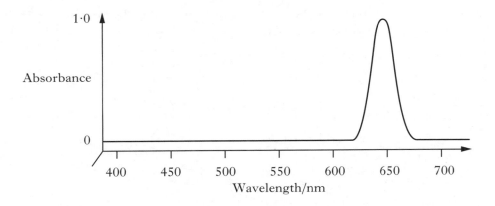

The absorption spectrum of a solution of sodium tetrachlorocobaltate(II) is shown above.

(a) Predict the most likely colour of the solution.   **1**

(b) Write the electronic configuration for a cobalt(II) ion in terms of s, p and d orbitals.   **1**

(c) Write the formula for the tetrachlorocobaltate(II) ion.   **1**

(3)

6. Propanoic acid is a weak acid. Sodium propanoate is a salt which can be formed from it. Both propanoic acid and sodium propanoate can be used as mould inhibitors.

(a) Calculate the pH of 0.10 mol l^{-1} propanoic acid solution.   **2**

(b) 0.20 moles of sodium propanoate are added to 100 cm^3 of the 0.10 mol l^{-1} solution of propanoic acid.

Calculate the pH of the buffer solution formed.   **2**

(4)

Marks

7. (*a*) Calculate the emf of a $Cr(s)|Cr^{3+}(aq)\|Fe^{2+}(aq)|Fe(s)$ cell operating under standard conditions. **1**

(*b*) Calculate the free energy change, $\Delta G°$, in kJ per mole of chromium, for this cell reaction. **3**

(*c*) Use the Ellingham diagram below to **explain** whether zinc or aluminium should be chosen to extract chromium from chromium oxide. **1**

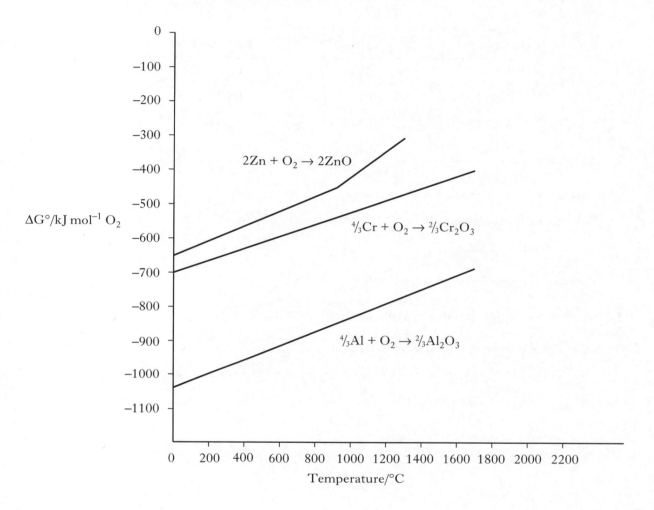

(5)

[Turn over

Marks

8. A kinetics study was carried out on the reaction between a halogenoalkane, C_4H_9Br, and aqueous sodium hydroxide.

$$C_4H_9Br + NaOH \rightarrow C_4H_9OH + NaBr$$

The following results were obtained.

$[C_4H_9Br]/mol\,l^{-1}$	$[NaOH]/mol\,l^{-1}$	Initial Rate/mol $l^{-1}s^{-1}$
8.0×10^{-4}	0·10	0·15
1.6×10^{-3}	0·10	0·30
1.6×10^{-3}	0·20	0·30
3.2×10^{-3}	0·40	0·60

(a) What is the order of reaction with respect to

   (i) the halogenoalkane

   (ii) the sodium hydroxide?   1

(b) Write the rate equation for the reaction.   1

(c) Calculate a value for the rate constant, k, including the appropriate units.   2

(d) There are four structural isomers of C_4H_9Br.

   (i) From the above results, which isomer is most likely to have been used?   1

   (ii) Explain your answer to (d)(i).   1

                                                                                                 (6)

9. Nickel(II) ions react quantitatively with dimethylglyoxime ($C_4H_8O_2N_2$) forming a complex which precipitates out as a red solid. The equation for the reaction and the structure of the complex are shown below.

$$Ni^{2+} + 2C_4H_8O_2N_2 \rightarrow Ni(C_4H_7O_2N_2)_2 + 2H^+$$

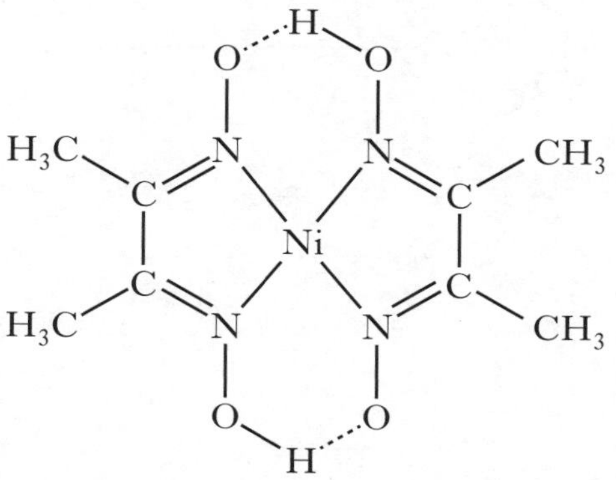

Relative formula mass = 288·7

(a) What is the coordination number of nickel in the complex?   1

(b) When 0·968 g of an impure sample of nickel(II) sulphate, $NiSO_4.7H_2O$, was dissolved in water and reacted with dimethylglyoxime, 0·942 g of the red precipitate was formed.

Calculate the percentage, by mass, of nickel in the impure sample of nickel(II) sulphate.   2

                                                                    (3)

[Turn over

Marks

10.   A student devised the following reaction sequence.

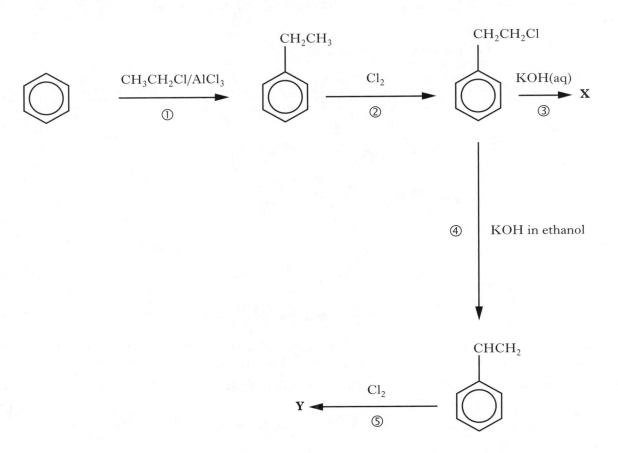

(a)   What type of reaction is taking place in step ①?   1

(b)   What experimental condition would be required in step ②?   1

(c)   Draw a structural formula for product **X**.   1

(d)   What type of reaction is taking place in step ④?   1

(e)   Draw a structural formula for product **Y**.   1

                                                                  (5)

Marks

11. Methylamphetamine (also known as "speed") and caffeine are stimulants.

A "designer drug" with a structure related to methylamphetamine is ecstasy. Ecstasy tablets are sometimes contaminated with a substance called 4-MTA.

methylamphetamine

caffeine

ecstasy

4-MTA

(a) Caffeine contains more than one "amide" functional group.

Draw the structure of caffeine and circle **one** of the "amide" functional groups.

1

(b) Which of the four molecules contains a primary amine functional group?

1

(c) Draw the structure of the pharmacaphore common to methylamphetamine, ecstasy and 4-MTA.

1

(3)

12. In a PPA, cyclohexene is prepared from cyclohexanol using a dehydrating agent.

(a) Which dehydrating agent is used in the PPA?

1

(b) (i) When the reactants have been heated gently for about 15 to 20 minutes, the mixture is allowed to cool. Separation of the product is carried out by adding saturated sodium chloride solution to the reaction mixture and vigorously shaking them together for about a minute and allowing them to settle and form two layers.

Why is saturated sodium chloride solution used rather than water?

1

(ii) Which piece of apparatus is used **in this part of the procedure**?

1

(c) The identity of the product can be verified by using infra-red spectroscopy.

Predict **one** difference that would be observed between the infra-red spectra of cyclohexene and cyclohexanol.

1

(4)

[Turn over

Marks

13. The diagram below shows a reaction sequence starting from compound **A** which is pentan-2-ol ($C_5H_{12}O$).

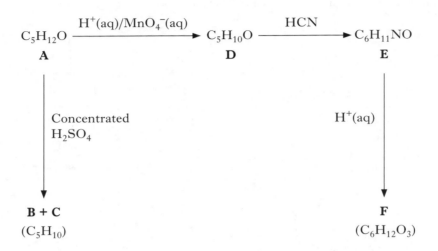

Compound **B** can exist as two geometric isomers.

Compound **C** is pent-1-ene.

Compound **D** is the oxidation product of compound **A**.

(a) Name **and** draw the structural formulae for the two geometric isomers of compound **B**.   2

(b) Name compound **D**.   1

(c) Compound **E** is a cyanohydrin.

  (i) Name the type of reaction occurring when **D** is converted into **E**.   1

  (ii) Draw a structural formula for compound **E**.   1

(d) Name **or** draw a structural formula for compound **F**.   1

    (6)

Marks

14. $5 \cdot 00$ g of an organic compound **A** was burned completely producing $11 \cdot 89$ g of CO_2 and $6 \cdot 08$ g of H_2O as the only products.

   (a)   **Using the information above**, calculate the empirical formula for compound **A**.   **3**

   (b)   The infra-red spectrum of compound **A** is shown below.

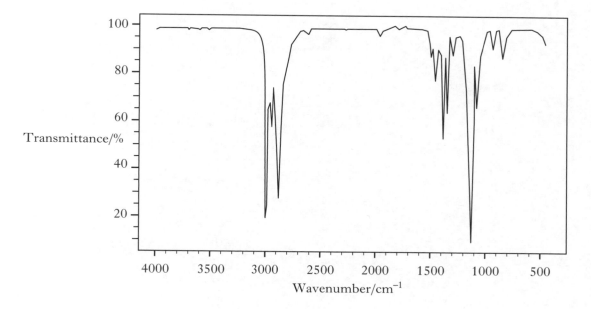

   Which bond is responsible for the peak at $1140 \, cm^{-1}$?   **1**

   (c)   The mass spectrum of compound **A** shows the molecular ion to have a mass/charge ratio of 74. Deduce the molecular formula of compound **A**.   **1**

   (d)   The proton nmr spectrum of compound **A** is shown below.

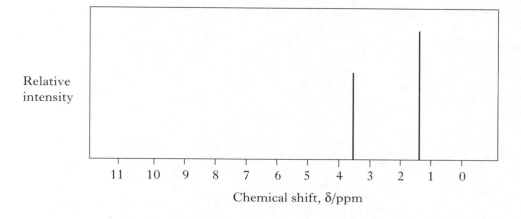

   Using all the above information, deduce the structural formula for compound **A**.   **1**

                                                                                    (6)

[END OF QUESTION PAPER]

[BLANK PAGE]

ADVANCED HIGHER | ANSWER SECTION

SQA ADVANCED HIGHER
CHEMISTRY 2009–2013

CHEMISTRY ADVANCED HIGHER
2009

SECTION A

1.	D	21.	B
2.	D	22.	C
3.	A	23.	A
4.	C	24.	C
5.	A	25.	B
6.	C	26.	D
7.	D	27.	D
8.	B	28.	A
9.	D	29.	C
10.	C	30.	C
11	D	31.	B
12.	D	32.	C
13.	A	33.	C
14.	A	34.	D
15.	B	35.	B
16.	C	36.	A
17.	A	37.	B
18.	A	38.	B
19.	D	39.	C
20.	B	40.	C

SECTION B

1. (a) $1s^2\ 2s^2\ 2p^6\ 3s^2\ 3p^6$

   (b) (i) E= 78.3 (nm)

   (ii) $Ar(g) \rightarrow Ar^+(g) + e^-$

2. (a) $138\ J\ K^{-1}\ mol^{-1}$

   (b) $96\ kJ\ mol^{-1}$

   (c) = 696 K

3. (a) $Mg^{2+}(aq)$

   (b) Lattice (breaking) enthalpy

   (c) $-728\ kJ$

   (d) $-322\ kJ\ mol^{-1}$

4. (a) Bond breaking H-H + $^1/_2$ (O=O)

   $= 432 + 248\cdot5 = 680\cdot5$
   Bond making 2 O-H = -916
   $\Delta H = (680\cdot5 - 916) = -235\cdot5\ (kJ\ mol^{-1})$

   (b) The above reaction has formed $H_2O(g)$ and more energy
   will be given out as it changes to $H_2O(l)$
   or
   Enthalpy of combustion forms $H_2O(l)$ at standard
   conditions but the above reaction has formed $H_2O(g)$

5. (a) $1\ mol\ l^{-1}\ H^+$ ions, 25°C (298K) and 1 atmosphere pressure

   (b) $2IO_3^- + 12H^+ + 10e^- \rightarrow I_2 + 6H_2O$

   (c) $-574\cdot2\ kJ\ mol^{-1}$

6. (a) (i) $HCOO^-$ **or** methanoate ion

   (ii) $K_a = \dfrac{[HCOO^-][H_3O^+]}{[HCOOH]}$

   (b) (i) $0\cdot0783\ mol\ l^{-1}$

   (ii) 2·43

7. (a) Rate = $k[CH_3COCH_3]\ [H^+]$

   (b) The H^+ is present at the **start** and the **end** of the reaction

   (c) (i) To quench/stop the reaction.
   To neutralise the acid.

   (ii) Starch solution **and** blue/black to colourless

8. (a) EDTA

   (b) nickel(II) ions are green **or** green/blue **or** coloured
   $Ni^{2+}(aq)$ absorb visible light

   (c) (i) it has lone pairs of electrons/non-bonding pairs of
   electrons

   (ii) 4

   (iii) gravimetric

   (iv) to prevent the complex from absorbing moisture
   or
   to allow the complex to cool in a dry atmosphere

9. (a)

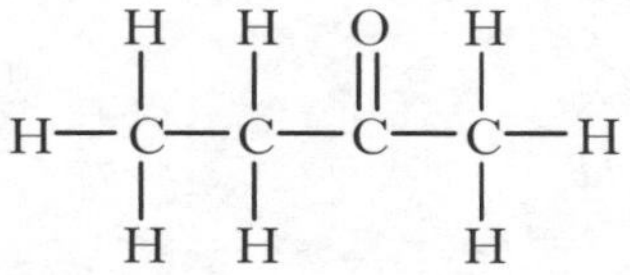

   or

   $CH_3CH_2COCH_3$

   (b) (nucleophilic) substitution

   (c) Find its melting point and check with literature values

   (d)

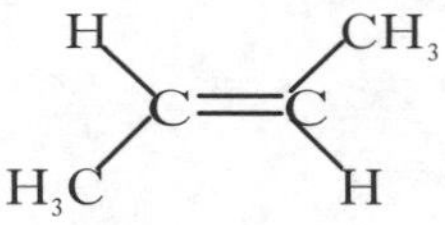

   trans-but-2-ene 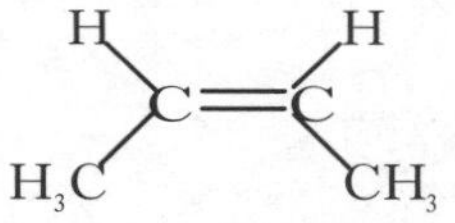   *cis*-but-2-ene

10. (a) H_2SO_4 and HNO_3
    or H_2SO_4 and $NaNO_3$

    (b) reduction

    (c) Ethanoic acid/CH_3COOH
    or ethanoyl chloride/CH_3COCl
    or ethanoic anhydride/$(CH_3CO)_2O$

11. (a) $C_4H_8O_2$

    (b) (i) carbonyl **or** C=O

    (ii) ester

    (c) $[CH_3CH_2CO]^+$
    $C_2H_5CO^+$

    (d) methyl propanoate

12. (a) +5 and +7

    (b) trigonal bipyramidal

    (c) sp^3d **or** sp^2d^2 **or** spd^3

    (d) Cl atom too small to accommodate 7 F atoms around it

13. (a)

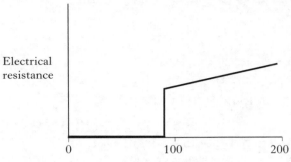

(b) (i)

	Y	Ba	Cu	O
mass/g	13·4	41·2	28·6	16·8
moles	$\frac{13·4}{88·9}$	$\frac{41·2}{137·3}$	$\frac{28·6}{63·5}$	$\frac{16·8}{16·0}$
	= 0·151	= 0·300	= 0·450	= 1·05
mole ratio	1	2	3	7

(ii) +2·33

(iii) $Y_2Ba_4Cu_6O_{13}$ **or** $YBa_2Cu_3O_6$

CHEMISTRY ADVANCED HIGHER 2010

SECTION A

1.	D	21.	D
2.	C	22.	C
3.	D	23.	C
4.	B	24.	A
5.	B	25.	C
6.	D	26.	D
7.	A	27.	C
8.	B	28.	B
9.	D	29.	A
10.	C	30.	B
11	C	31.	D
12.	A	32.	B
13.	B	33.	A
14.	A	34.	B
15.	D	35.	D
16.	A	36.	A
17.	D	37.	C
18.	B	38.	B
19.	C	39.	A
20.	D	40.	C

SECTION B

1. (a) $E = \dfrac{Lhc}{\lambda}$ **or** $\dfrac{Lhc}{1000\lambda}$

$$E = \frac{6·02 \times 10^{23} \times 6·63 \times 10^{-34} \times 3·00 \times 10^8}{160 \times 10^{-9}}$$

$E = 748$ (kJ mol^{-1}) **or** 748361J

(b) (i) 5
(ii) trigonal bipyramidal

2. (a) +3 **or** III **or** 3

(b) tetraaquadichlorochromium(III)

(c)

3. (a) $\Delta H° = (-1676) - (-824) = $ **−852 kJ**

(b) $\Delta S° = [2(27) + 51] - [2(28) + 87] = $ **−38 JK^{-1}**

(c) $\Delta G° = \Delta H° - T\Delta S° = (-852) - 298(-38/1000)$
$= -852 + 11·32 = $ **−841kJ**

4. (a) (i) Brown fumes, fizzing, solution turning yellow, NO$_2$ forming
(ii) Oxidising agent
(iii) Max absorbance of permanganate/Green is the complementary colour of purple

(b) moles of Mn = $1.4 \times 10^{-4} \times 0.1$
$$= \mathbf{1.4 \times 10^{-5}}$$
mass of Mn = $1.4 \times 10^{-5} \times 54.9$
$$= \mathbf{7.686 \times 10^{-4}\ g}$$
% Mm = $(7.686 \times 10^{-4} / 0.19) \times 100$
$$= \mathbf{0.40\%}$$

5. (a)

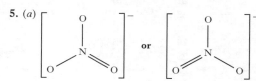

(b) b = 0
c = −1 and d = −1

6. (a) (i) colourless to pink/colourless to purple
(ii) $(16.5/1000) \times 0.02 \times 5/2 = \mathbf{0.000825 moles}$
(8.25×10^{-4})
(iii) $0.000825 \times (1000/20) \times 88 = \mathbf{3.63g}$
(iv) $4.49 - 3.63 - 0.06 = \mathbf{0.8g}$

(b)
K	H	C_2O_4
0.8/39	0.06/1	3.63/88
0.020	0.060	0.041

X = 1   Y = 3   Z = 2

7. (a)
$$CH_3CH_2OH + CH_3COOH \rightleftharpoons CH_3COOCH_2CH_3 + H_2O$$

(b) (i) No equilibrium in open system/System will not reach equilibrium
(ii) At equilibrium:
moles of water and ester = $0.70 - 0.24 = \mathbf{0.46}$
moles of ethanoic acid = 0.24
moles of ethanol = $0.68 - 0.46 = \mathbf{0.22}$
K = [0.46][0.46]/[0.24][0.22] = **4.0**

8. (a)

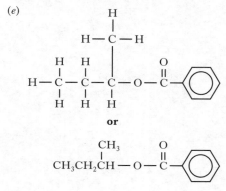

(b) pKa = −logKa = −log 1.4×10^{-5} = 4.85
pH = ½ pKa − ½ logc
Substitute values   3.77 = 2.43 − ½ logc
c = 0.0020mol l⁻¹

9. (a) Step two
or
NO_2 + F → NO_2F
(b) $2NO_2$ + F_2 → $2NO_2F$
or
NO_2 + ½F_2 → NO_2F

(c) 2nd order **or** 2

(d) k = Initial rate/[NO₂][F₂] = **40 ℓ mol ⁻¹s⁻¹**

10. (a) to give a higher yield
or
to reduce side reactions
or
to prevent charring

(b) sodium chloride (solution)/brine/salt water

(c) to dry the cyclohexene/dry the organic layer/drying agent/absorbs water/removes water

(d) Theoretical mass
of cyclohexene $= \dfrac{82 \times 22.56}{100} = 18.5\ g$
% yield $= \dfrac{6.52 \times 100}{18.5} = 35\ \%$
or
Moles cyclohexanol = 22.56/100 = 0.2256 mol
Moles cyclohexane = 6.52/82 = 0.0795 mol
% yield $= \dfrac{0.0795}{0.2256} \times 100 = 35.2\ \%$ **or**   35%

11. (a) because but-2-ene has two different groups attached to each of the carbon atoms of the double bond
or
because in but-1-ene one of the carbon atoms of the double bond has identical groups (H) attached

(b)

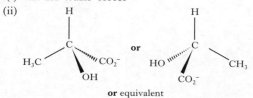

(c) aqueous potassium (or sodium) hydroxide KOH(aq) or NaOH(aq) or LiOH(aq)
or
potassium (or sodium) hydroxide solution
or
aqueous alkali
or
alkali solution
or
water/H_2O

(d) aluminium chloride or $AℓCℓ_3$
or
iron(III) chloride or $FeCℓ_3$
or
iron(III) bromide or $FeBr_3$
or
aluminium bromide or $AℓBr_3$

(e)

(H–C–H structure)

or

CH_3CH_2CH — O — C(=O)–phenyl

12. (a) ethanal

(b) cyanohydrin

(c) hydrolysis/acid hydrolysis

(d) (i) van der Waals' forces
(ii)

or equivalent

Must be tetrahedral but dots and wedges can be replaced by solid lines

(iii) while one group would be able to bind to the appropriate region, the other two would not

or

the 3 'functional' groups fail to match the binding regions of the active site

or

only 1 group or 2 groups could bind (or match) the binding regions

or

The groups on the lactate ion no longer match the binding regions on the active site of the enzyme

or

The lactate ion no longer complements the binding region (of the active site)

or

The groups now fail to match the binding region (of the active site)

13. (a) Alcohols or alkanols

   and

   ethers

   (b) (i)

   $$H-\underset{\underset{H}{|}}{\overset{\overset{H}{|}}{C}}-\underset{}{\overset{\overset{O}{\|}}{C}}-\underset{\underset{H}{|}}{\overset{\overset{H}{|}}{C}}-\underset{\underset{H}{|}}{\overset{\overset{H}{|}}{C}}-H \quad \textbf{or} \quad CH_3COCH_2CH_3$$

   (ii) butan-2-ol

CHEMISTRY ADVANCED HIGHER 2011

SECTION A

1.	A	21.	B
2.	B	22.	A
3.	A	23.	D
4.	C	24.	B
5.	C	25.	D
6.	C	26.	C
7.	A	27.	A
8.	D	28.	C
9.	C	29.	A
10.	D	30.	C
11.	B	31.	A
12.	C	32.	B
13.	A	33.	D
14.	C	34.	B
15.	C	35.	D
16.	D	36.	B
17.	B	37.	C
18.	B	38.	A
19.	A	39.	D
20.	D	40.	D

SECTION B

1. (a) Superconductivity
   Superconducting
   Superconductor
   Superconductance

   (b) Liquid nitrogen/N_2

2. (a) The line at $4 \cdot 6 \times 10^{14}$ Hz

   (b) (i) $H(g) \rightarrow H^+(g) + e^-$
       $H(g) - e^- \rightarrow H^+(g)$

   (ii) $E = \dfrac{Lhc}{\lambda}$ **or** $E = \dfrac{Lhc}{1000\lambda}$

   Wavelength, $\lambda = \dfrac{6\cdot02 \times 10^{23} \times 6\cdot63 \times 10^{-34} \times 3\cdot00 \times 10^8}{1311000}$

   $= 91\cdot3 \times 10^{-9}$ m **or** $91\cdot3$ nm **or** $9\cdot13 \times 10^{-8}$ m

   or 91 nm

3. (a) In NO, oxidation state is 2 or +2 or II **or** 2+
   In NO_2, oxidation state is 4 or +4 or IV **or** 4+

   (b)

   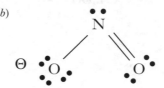

   (c) $NO_2^-(aq) + H_2O(l) \rightarrow NO_3^-(aq) + 2H^+(aq) + 2e^-$

4. (a) (i) Fe^{3+} $1s^22s^22p^63s^23p^63d^5$
       (ii) Mn^{3+} $1s^22s^22p^63s^23p^63d^4$
       (iii) Fe^{3+} has half filled d-subshell
            or All d-orbitals half filled in Fe^{3+}

   (b) Moles of $FeTiO_3 = 3250/151\cdot7 = \mathbf{21\cdot42}$
       Mass of $TiO_2 = n \times FM = 21\cdot42 \times 79\cdot9 = 1711$ g = **1·71 kg**

   (c) $(NH_4)_2[Cu(Cl)_4]$

5. (a) Step 4: Rinse beaker with deionised water, add washings to standard flask.
       Step 5: Add deionised water up to mark on standard flask.

   (b) (i) Murexide or ammonium purpurate
       (ii) Octahedral

(iii) Average titre = 23·55 cm^3

No of moles of Ni in 100 cm^3 solution
= 0·02355 × 0·110 × 4 = 0·0104

% mass of Ni = $\dfrac{0·0104 \times 58·7}{2·656} \times 100$ = **22·98%**

6. (a) T = 300 − 310 K

(b) $\Delta H° = 380 - (420)$ (kJ mol^{-1})

(c) Gradient of line = −1·3 (kJ K^{-1} mol^{-1})
or $\Delta S° = 1·22$ to
1·40 kJ K^{-1} mol^{-1}

$\Delta S° = (+) 1220$ to 1400 (J K^{-1} mol^{-1})

7. (a) Third order/3rd/3

(b) Reaction 3
Rate is independent of concentration of reactants

or rate is independent of concentration of ammonia

or Concentration of reactant has no effect on rate

(c) k = $\dfrac{Rate}{[NO]^2[Cl_2]}$ = $\dfrac{1·43 \times 10^{-6}}{(0·250)^2(0·250)}$

= **9·15 × 10^{-5} l^2 mol^{-2} s^{-1}**

8. (a) $H_2O_2(aq) + 2H^+(aq) + 2Br^-(aq) \rightarrow Br_2(l) + 2H_2O(l)$

(b) $\Delta G° = -nFE°$
$= -2 \times 96500 \times 0·70$
$= -135·1$ kJ mol^{-1}

9. (a) A solution in which the pH remains (approximately) constant when small amounts of acid, alkali or water are added, or a solution which resists pH changes when acid/alkali added

(b) Sodium propanoate or potassium propanoate

(c) [salt] = $\dfrac{0·15/80·0}{0·1}$ = 0·131 mol l^{-1}

pH = 14 − 4·76 + log $\dfrac{0·15}{0·131}$

pH = 14 − 4·76 + 0·059 = **9·30**

10. (a) Pharmacaphore

(b)

11. (a)

C	H	O
$\frac{50}{12}$	$\frac{5·6}{1}$	$\frac{44·4}{16}$
4·16	5·6	2·77
1·50	2·02	1

giving C$_3$H$_4$O$_2$

(b) (i) C$_6$H$_8$O$_4$

(ii) 2500 − 3500 (cm^{-1})
or 1700 − 1725 cm^{-1}

12. (a) Condensation

(b)

(c) (i)

(ii) Crystallisation/recrystallisation

(iii) Measure melting point **and** compare to known data/value

(iv) Yellow **or** orange **or** gold

13. (a) (i) Nucleophilic substitution/replacement by a nucleophile
First order **or** unimolecular

(ii)

(b) (i) Na in ethanol

(ii) Methoxyethane

14. (a) 2-hydroxypropanoic acid

(b) Carbon atom ② because it has 4 different groups attached

(c) (i) KCN or NaCN or HCN
or correct names

(ii) Hydrolysis/acid hydrolysis

(iii)

or CH$_2$CHOHCH$_2$NH$_2$

CHEMISTRY ADVANCED HIGHER 2012

SECTION A

1.	A	21.	C
2.	D	22.	C
3.	D	23.	B
4.	A	24.	D
5.	B	25.	B
6.	B	26.	A
7.	D	27.	C
8.	C	28.	D
9.	C	29.	A
10.	A	30.	B
11.	C	31.	B
12.	D	32.	A
13.	D	33.	B
14.	B	34.	D
15.	A	35.	B
16.	A	36.	B
17.	A	37.	D
18.	C	38.	A
19.	C	39.	D
20.	D	40.	D

SECTION B

1. (a) (i) $E = \dfrac{Lhc}{\lambda}$

$$= \frac{(6\cdot02 \times 10^{23}) \times (6\cdot63 \times 10^{-34}) \times (3\cdot00 \times 10^{8})}{1000 \times 405 \ 10^{-9}}$$

$$= 296 \ (kJ \ mol^{-1})$$

   (ii) $1s^2 \ 2s^2 2p^6 \ 3s^2 3p^6 3d^{10}$

   (b) Photovoltaic effect

   (c) Positive holes

2. (a) (i) 5 **or** V **or** (V)

   (ii) 3 **or** III **or** (III)

   (b) $2HNO_2 + 4H^+ + 4e^- \rightarrow H_2N_2O_2 + 2H_2O$

   (c) Dicyanocuprate(I)

3. (a) The relative radii of the ions.
      The relative size of the ions.
      The radius ratio of the ions.

   (b) Each sodium ion has six chloride ions surrounding it and each chloride ion has six sodium ions surrounding it.

   (c) Potassium fluoride

   (d) (i) lattice enthalpy and hydration enthalpies (of the ions)

   (ii) The entropy change is positive/positive entropy/ increase in entropy/increase in disorder / ΔS positive

4. (a) Trigonal planar

   (b) Oxygen donates a lone pair of electrons to boron
      or
      correct idea that both electrons have come from the oxygen

   (c) Cyclic ethers or ether(s) or furans or cycloethers

5. (a) No of moles thiosulphate $= 15.25 \times 0.102/1000$
      $= 1.56 \times 10^{-3}$ so moles $Cu^{2+} = 1.56 \times 10^{-3}$

   Mass Cu per sample $= 63.5 \times 1.56 \times 10^{-3} = 9.88 \times 10^{-2}$

   Mass of Cu in key $= 9.88 \times 10^{-2} \times 1000/25 =$ **3.95g**

   (b) Use distilled/deionised water.
      Start with different samples from the key and carry out replicates / duplicates.

   (c) EDTA complexes with Cu as well as Ni

6. (a) Separating funnel/separation funnel/separatory funnel

   (b) 0.127 — 0.130

   (c) Different temperature
      One of the solutions may be saturated

   (d) Ethanol and water are miscible
      Ethanol soluble in water
      Two layers won't be formed

7. (a) $pH = \frac{1}{2}pK_a - \frac{1}{2}\log c$ **or** $c = \dfrac{\sqrt{[H^+]^2}}{Ka}$

      or

      $2.5 = \frac{1}{2} \times 4.76 - \frac{1}{2}\log c$ $= \dfrac{\sqrt{(10^{-2.5})^2}}{1.7 \times 10^{-5}}$

      $c =$ **5.75×10^{-1}** $mol \ l^{-1}$ $=$ **0.575** $mol \ l^{-1}$
      $(0.575 \ mol \ l^{-1})$ $(0.588 \ mol \ l^{-1})$

   (b) Because of the (dark) colour of vinegar or words to that effect, eg the colour change would be hard to see

   (c) CH_3COO^- **or** correct structural formula or $C_2H_3O_2^-$

8. (a) "Temperatures **below** 2000 K"
      or 0 – 2000 K

   (b) Slope of line is- ΔS
      or
      $2C + O_2 \rightarrow 2CO$ has increase in entropy
      or
      1 mole gas makes two moles gas
      or
      increase in disorder
      or
      ΔS is positive

   (c) Boiling point of Mg/Change of state/magnesium becomes a gas

9. $\Delta G = -nFE^\circ$ **or** $E^\circ = \dfrac{-\Delta G}{nF}$

   $\dfrac{279.8 \times 10^3}{2 \times 96,500}$

   $= $ **1.45** V(olts)

10. (a) Zero **or** 0

    (b) First **or** 1

    (c) s^{-1}

11. (a) (i) Hydrogen or H_2

    (ii) Hydrogen chloride or HCl

    (b) (i) acid chloride, acyl chloride

    (ii)

$C_6H_5COOCH(CH_3)_2$

    (iii) Faster reaction/ More vigorous reaction/greater yield/needs no catalyst/no equilibrium reached (in an open system)

12. (a) $C_8H_{14}S_2O_2$

(b) (i) The carbon atom where the tail joins the ring.

(ii) It has four different atoms or groups (substituents) attached to it.
The "tail" and hydrogen atom attached to that carbon atom can each be in front of or behind the plane of the ring.

13. (a) To prevent evaporation or idea of products or reactant or gases or chemicals escaping
To reduce smell.

(b) (Alkaline) hydrolysis/hydrolysing

(c) A few glass beads or anti-bumping granules.

(d) The oily layer disappears/no longer two layers/goes clear/no more oily droplets/cloudy to colourless

(e) $C_6H_5COOC_2H_5$ (150 g) → C_6H_5COOH (122 g)
5.64 g → **4.59** g
73.2 % of 4.59 g = **3.36** g
or
Using mol calculation, then get 0.0275 mol
Final answer = 3.36 g (as before)

14. (a) (i) Electrophilic substitution

(ii) Aminobenzene/Phenylamine/Aniline
or correct (structural) formula/$C_6H_5NH_2$

(b) (i)

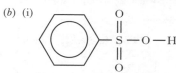

(ii)

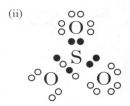

15. (a) $CH_3CH_2CHClCH_3$

or

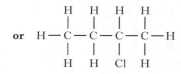

(b)

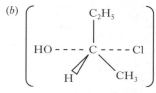

(c)

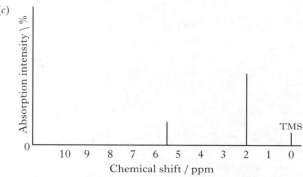

Lines can be between 4.5–6.0 and 1.6–2.6 ppm but line of lower chemical shift should be 3× height of other line.

CHEMISTRY ADVANCED HIGHER 2013

SECTION A

1.	C	21.	B
2.	B	22.	D
3.	A	23.	A
4.	D	24.	B
5.	D	25.	B
6.	A	26.	C
7.	C	27.	B
8.	A	28.	D
9.	C	29.	D
10.	B	30.	A
11.	C	31.	D
12.	C	32.	A
13.	D	33.	B
14.	B	34.	D
15.	A	35.	D
16.	C	36.	C
17.	B	37.	D
18.	C	38.	B
19.	A	39.	A
20.	D	40.	D

SECTION B

1. (a) Any group 3 element,
or boron, aluminium, gallium, indium or thallium
or **correct** symbol

(b) Positive hole(s)
+ve holes
Electron deficient holes

2. (a) -220.3 J K^{-1} (mol^{-1}) or -0.2203 kJ K^{-1} (mol^{-1})

(b) $\Delta H° = -592$ (kJ mol^{-1})

$\Delta G° = \Delta H° - T\Delta S°$

$= -526.35$ kJ (mol^{-1})

3. (a) Rb(s) + ½ Cl_2(g) → Rb$^+$Cl$^-$(s) (or RbCl(s))

(b) -349 kJ mol^{-1} or -349 kJ

(c) Lattice (formation) enthalpy
Lattice energy

(d) -697.5 kJ (mol^{-1})

4. (a) A series of standard solutions of different concentrations of $KMnO_4$ is made up and their absorbances measured. Absorbances of permanganate solutions of known concentrations/variety of concentrations
(must mention permanganate or manganate solutions)

(b) Green or 500 to 560 nm

(c) Nitrogen dioxide/dinitrogen tetroxide/nitrogen monoxide/nitric oxide.
or correct formulae eg NO, NO_2, N_2O_4

(d) E = $\dfrac{Lhc}{\lambda}$ or E = $\dfrac{Lhc}{1000\lambda}$

$= 296$ or 295.6 or 295.65 (kJ mol^{-1})

5. (a) Blue or green or blue/green

(b) $1s^2\ 2s^2\ 2p^6\ 3s^2\ 3p^6\ 3d^7$ or correct answer in terms of orbital box notation with all the orbitals labelled correctly

(c) [Co(Cl)$_4$]$^{2-}$ or [CoCl$_4$]$^{2-}$ or CoCl$_4$$^{2-}$

6. (a) $pH = \frac{1}{2} pK_a - \frac{1}{2} \log c$

$= 2.935$ or 2.94 or 2.9

(b) $pH = pK_a - \log \dfrac{[\text{acid}]}{[\text{salt}]}$

$= 6.171$ or 6.17 or 6.2

7. (a) Emf $= 0.74 - 0.44 = 0.30$ V or 0.3 V

(b) $\Delta G° = -nFE°$
$= -3 \times 96500 \times 0.3$ (J per mole Cr)
$= -86.9$ (kJ per mole Cr)

(c) Aluminium because $\Sigma\Delta G°$ is negative for the reactions
$2/3\ Cr_2O_3 \quad \rightarrow \quad 4/3Cr + O_2$
$+ 4/3Al + O_2 \rightarrow \quad 2/3Al_2O_3$
or
Overall $\Delta G°$ is negative for the (redox) reaction:

$2/3Cr_2O_3 + 4/3Al \rightarrow 4/3Cr + 2/3Al_2O_3$

8. (a) (i) First or 1

(ii) Zero or 0

(b) Rate $= k[C_4H_9Br]$

(c) $k = Rate/[C_4H_9Br] = 0.15/8.0 \times 10^{-4} = 187.5$ s^{-1}

(d) (i) 2-bromomethylpropane or 2-bromo-2-methylpropane

(ii) Correct explanation in terms of stability of carbocation or Steric hindrance

9. (a) 4 or four

(b) Mass of nickel in DMG complex

$= 0.942 \times (58.7/288.7) = 0.1915$ g or 0.192 g

% Ni in impure salt $= (0.1915/0.968) \times 100 = 19.8$ (%)

10. (a) Electrophilic substitution
or
Alkylation

(b) Light/UV radiation/radiation of correct wavelength

(c)
CH$_2$ CH$_2$ OH

(d) (base induced) elimination,

(e)
or
$C_6H_5CHClCH_2Cl$

11. (a)

Caffeine

Any one of the three amide functional groups circled above

(b) 4-MTA

(c)

12. (a) (Concentrated) phosphoric acid/orthophosphoric acid

(b) (i) It is denser than water.

(ii) Separating funnel/separatory funnel/separation funnel

(c) Presence of:
C=C stretch/1620 to 1680 cm^{-1} in **cyclohexene**.
C–H stretch or/ 3095 to 3010 cm^{-1} in **cyclohexene**.
O–H stretch or/ 3200 to 3650 cm^{-1} in **cyclohexanol**.

13. (a)

cis-pent-2-ene

trans-pent-2-ene

(b) Pentan-2-one.

(c) (i) (nucleophilic) addition.

(ii)

(d) 2-hydroxy-2-methylpentanoic acid

or

14. (*a*) Mass of C = $(12/44 \times 11 \cdot 89) = 3 \cdot 243$ g

Mass of H = $(2/18 \times 6 \cdot 08) = 0 \cdot 676$ g

So mass of O = $5 \cdot 00 - 3 \cdot 243 - 0 \cdot 676 = 1 \cdot 081$ g

$$C \ : \ H \ : \ O$$
$$3 \cdot 243 \ : \ 0 \cdot 676 \ : \ 1 \cdot 081$$

Ratio of moles $0 \cdot 270 \ : \ 0 \cdot 676 \ : \ 0 \cdot 0676$

$$4 \ : \ 10 \ : \ 1$$

Empirical formula $C_4H_{10}O$

(*b*) C-O (stretch)

(*c*) $C_4H_{10}O$

(*d*)

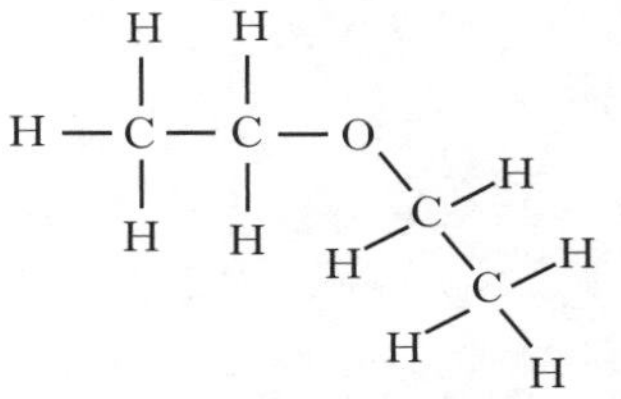